FOREWORD TO THE 1993 REPRINT

The *International Classification of Impairments, Disabilities, and Handicaps* (ICIDH), developed in the 1970s, was issued by the World Health Organization in 1980 as a tool for the classification of the consequences of disease (as well as of injuries and other disorders) and of their implications for the lives of individuals. It now exists in 13 languages[1] and further versions in other languages are in preparation; more than 15 000 copies of the English and French versions and over 10 000 copies in other languages have been distributed. The bibliography maintained by the WHO Collaborating Centre on ICIDH in the Netherlands lists over 1000 references to the ICIDH. Published comments on the ICIDH include such remarks as: "[The ICIDH] concepts provide the key to rational management of chronic diseases"; at the same time, however, concern has been expressed that the ICIDH does not state clearly enough the role of social and physical environment in the process of handicap, and that it might be construed as encouraging "the medicalization of disablement". (The term "disablement" is used here to encompass the full range of impairment, disability, and handicap.)

The ICIDH belongs to the "family" of classifications developed by WHO for application to various aspects of health and disease. The best established is the *International Statistical Classification of Diseases, Injuries, and Causes of Death* (ICD), the Ninth Revision of which (ICD–9) was issued shortly before the publication of the ICIDH. The first volume of the Tenth Revision of the ICD (ICD–10), published in June 1992, includes various changes, for instance in the area of mental and behavioural disorders, which will have to be taken into account in a revised ICIDH.

The dissemination and application of the ICIDH, as well as the advocacy role of organizations and bodies devoted to the problems of people with disabilities, have been accompanied by important changes in the way impairments, disabilities, and handicaps, and the various problems that may arise in each of these three areas are perceived and addressed. The listing of the classification items has allowed a better description and facilitated the assessment of people with disabilities and of their situation within a given physical and social environment.

This foreword is intended to clarify certain aspects of the 1980 introduction which have been the subject of much discussion, and to indicate some of the issues to be addressed in a forthcoming revision. It also offers an opportunity to provide information on the range of uses of the ICIDH and on the developments that have occurred as a result of its publication. In other respects, the manual is essentially unchanged and includes the original introduction.

Two Collaborating Centres for the ICIDH have been established, in France (*Centre technique national d'Etudes et de Recherches sur les Handicaps et les Inadaptations*) and in the Netherlands (Standing Committee for Classifications and Terminology). Together with other WHO Collaborating Centres for Health-related Classifications, notably those in

---

[1] A list of translations is available on request from Strengthening of Epidemiological and Statistical Services (SES/HST), World Health Organization, 1211 Geneva 27, Switzerland.

Uppsala, Sweden, for the Nordic countries, and at the National Center for Health Statistics, Hyattsville, MD, USA for North America, with groups such as the Canadian Society for the ICIDH and the *Réseau pour l'Etude de l'Espérance de Vie en Santé/International Network on the Study of Healthy Life Expectancy* (REVES), and with intergovernmental organizations such as the Statistical Division of the United Nations Department of Social and Economic Development, and the Council of Europe, these Centres have formed a technical network which has been in operation since 1987. The Council of Europe has established a Committee of Experts for the Application of the WHO International Classification of Impairments, Disabilities, and Handicaps, which brings together representatives of 14 countries, plus five observers. This Committee has examined specific applications of the ICIDH in rehabilitation work, surveys, and the collection of statistics, in the study of mental retardation, the assessment of vocational capacity, the assessment of technical enabling devices, and the application of the concept of handicap. The *Real Patronato de Prevención y de Atención a Personas con Minusvalía* in Madrid has undertaken a survey of the use of the ICIDH in Spanish-speaking countries.

Current applications of the ICIDH

The ICIDH is intended to offer a conceptual framework for information; the framework is relevant to the long-term consequences of disease, injuries, or disorders, and applicable both to personal health care, including early identification and prevention, and to the mitigation of environmental and societal barriers. It is also relevant to the study of health care systems, in terms both of evaluation and of policy formulation. The concepts of the ICIDH have elicited much philosophical interest, and its applications have covered activities in social security, the design of population surveys at local, national, and international levels, and other areas, such as the assessment of working capacities, demography, community needs assessment, town planning, and architecture. Although the ICIDH is inherently a health-related classification, future documentation and development will need to reflect a broader spectrum of applications and users.

A primary application of the ICIDH has been in describing the circumstances of individuals with disabilities across a wide range of settings. The ICIDH has been directly applied to the care of individuals in diagnosis and treatment, evaluation of treatment results, assessment for work, and information. Reports on its use in personal health care have come from nurses, occupational therapists, physicians, physiotherapists and others working with a wide variety of people, including elderly people, children and adolescents, and psychiatric patients, in many widely different countries, including Australia, the Netherlands, Pakistan, Spain, Venezuela, and Zimbabwe. The ICIDH is also used to assess patients in rehabilitation, in nursing homes, and in homes for the elderly; its use in these areas has facilitated communication between various categories of workers and coordination between different types of care.

CONTENTS

International Classification of Impairments, Disabilities, and Handicaps

A manual of classification
relating to the
consequences of disease

Published in accordance with
resolution WHA29.35 of the Twenty-ninth World Health Assembly,
May 1976

WORLD HEALTH ORGANIZATION
GENEVA
1980

Reprinted 1985, 1989, 1993 (with foreword

RY

USE

ISBN 92 4 154126 1

PRINTED IN USA

79/4624 – 84/6287 – 89/8176 – 92/9504 – 12500
94/9968 – Boyd – 3000

At the institutional level the ICIDH has been used to assess the numbers and type of staff required, and to study discharge policies and the characteristics of health-care utilization. At the community level, it has helped in identifying the needs of people with disabilities and handicaps, identifying handicapping situations in the social and physical environment, and formulating the policy decisions necessary for improvements in everyday life, including modifications of the physical and social environment.

In the areas of social security, occupational health, and employment, the ICIDH serves as an actual or potential basis for various assessments: for decisions on allowances, the orientation of individuals, and the nomenclature of handicaps in France, for the assessment of working abilities in Germany and the Netherlands, and for access to institutional care and to enabling devices in Italy and in Belgium (by the Flemish Fund for the Social Integration of Persons with a Handicap). Switzerland is investigating the use of the ICIDH in health insurance nomenclature.

The framework of the ICIDH has been used successfully by demographers, epidemiologists, health planners, policy-makers, and statisticians in disability surveys at national, regional, and local levels in several countries, both developed (*inter alia* Australia, Canada, Netherlands) and developing (*inter alia* Algeria, China, Fiji, Kuwait). Definitions used in the ICIDH have also served as a basis for surveys in the Netherlands, the United Kingdom, and most notably Spain, and for analysis of survey results. The statistical tools developed by the Statistical Division of the United Nations Department of Social and Economic Development for the international monitoring of population and household censuses, surveys, and administrative systems include an *International Disability Statistics Database* (DISTAT), which uses a framework based on the ICIDH; DISTAT covers national statistics from over 95 countries both in machine-readable form and as a printed *Compendium on Disability*. ICIDH concepts and definitions have been similarly used to determine various types of demographic indicators of Healthy Life Expectancy (impairment-free, disability-free, or handicap-free life expectancy) for a range of developing and developed countries. The use of the ICIDH in surveys has highlighted the relationships between impairment and disability and between disability and handicap; indeed, whether a survey is based on the concept of impairment or on that of disability can lead to marked differences in the resulting assessment of the population.

At the conceptual and policy levels, the use of the ICIDH has changed the ways in which disabilities themselves, people with disabilities, and the role of the physical and social environment in the development of handicap are considered. It has also changed some of the policy, planning, and administrative reactions of governments, organizations, and individuals to these concepts. The action taken by France in the promotion of an adapted version of the ICIDH for the collection of data on social services, and in the application of a *Nomenclature des handicaps* based on the ICIDH can be taken as one example (similar action is being considered in other countries); recent legislation in Italy is another. In Quebec, Canada, a systematic approach to policies on impairment, disability, and handicap is largely based on the ICIDH. Active interest in the ICIDH has recently been demonstrated in the USA, during and after the preparation of the *Americans with Disabilities Act* and in the publication of a major report on *Disability in America*. Even by those who do not necessarily accept it as the dominant framework, the ICIDH is widely recognized as an important standard for a conceptual framework in this field.

Some problems identified in the use of the ICIDH

An important task in the revision of the ICIDH will be to clarify the role and interrelationships of environmental factors in the definition and development of the different aspects addressed by the ICIDH, most notably – but not exclusively – handicap. A report of the united Nations Commission on Human Rights for its Forty-third Session on Human Rights and Disability encouraged WHO to revise the ICIDH and to consider more specifically the role of the environment in the development of the handicap process. Much work has addressed conceptual developments for this topic, notably the proposals issued by the Canadian Society for the ICIDH on the development of the handicap process. The role of the social and physical environment is briefly addressed in the original introduction to the ICIDH (see page 14):

> **"Handicap is more problematical. The structure of the Handicap classification is radically different from all other ICD-related classifications. The items are not classified according to individuals or their attributes but rather according to the circumstances in which people with disabilities are likely to find themselves, circumstances that can be expected to place such individuals at a disadvantage in relation to their peers when viewed from the norms of society."**

This will require elaboration in the revised version. The Handicap classification is a classification of situations and not of individuals: the word "circumstances" is to be considered as referring not only to statistical aggregates of individuals, but also to characteristics of the physical and social environment. Indicators for both categories are also under development in the field of health promotion.

The categories of impairment, disability, and handicap remain robust; non-ICIDH-based models embody similar concepts, although they may use different terms. A number of models of the consequences of disease which incorporate other factors, such as the physical and social environment, have been proposed in the scientific literature, and will be considered during revision of the ICIDH, although most remain at the stage of theoretical development and empirical testing.

In several instances, there is a degree of overlap between disability and handicap as regards functional limitations and activities of daily living. This overlap also occurs between impairment and disability, for instance as regards: intellectual impairments; the distinction between aural, ocular, and language impairments and communication disabilities; incontinence; and physical independence. The problem of overlap will require further elaboration.

The current model of the consequences of disease and its graphic representation (see page 30) are effective in distinguishing between impairments, disabilities, and handicaps as separate concepts, but do not provide adequate information on the relationship between them. In particular, the arrows linking disease or disorder, impairment, disability, and handicap have occasionally been interpreted as representing a causal model and an indication of change over time. This representation does not allow for movement from handicap and disability back to impairment, as facilitated by appropriate interventions, and has thus been taken to imply a unidirectional flow from impairment, to disability, to handicap. Furthermore, the graphic representation of the ICIDH framework does not adequately reflect the role of the social and physical environment in the handicap process. Although the original text states that the situation is more complex than a simple linear progression, this statement needs to be made more clearly — the arrows in the graphic presentation must be understood as meaning no more than "may lead to". These issues, as well as alternative graphic representations, will be considered in the revision of the ICIDH.

Some proposed changes to the ICIDH

The ICIDH has found a wider range of uses and users than was originally envisaged. Its value as a tool for planners and policy-makers has been amply demonstrated, notably in Canada and France, and this aspect should be stressed and extended in an introductory section of the revised version. Similar considerations apply to other facets of its use. Several reports comment that the ICIDH is not difficult to use, and this is encouraging; in an effort to broaden the application of the classification, revision should tend towards simplification rather than towards the addition of further detail. Revision, particularly of the impairment classification, must also take into account the needs of users who are not health professionals; for example, the revised version should include alphabetical indexes in addition to the index that now exists for impairments only. Consideration should also be given to the problem of application in specific population groups (e.g. children, because their status changes rapidly), and more space should be given to the problems of measurement of severity; the guidance and rulings on this included in the current version will be reconsidered.

In view of the concern about the way in which the definition of handicap is presented and understood, suggestions for revision include greater emphasis on presenting handicap as a description of the circumstances that individuals encounter as a result of interaction between their impairments or disabilities and their physical and social environment. An important task in the revision of the ICIDH will be to improve the presentation and illustration of the way in which external factors affect the ICIDH components. The introduction must stress the importance of the environment, together with the role and interaction of both individual characteristics and physical and social factors.

However, these factors, which are major components of the handicap process, should not be developed as an additional classification scheme within the ICIDH. Social and physical factors in the environment, and their relationship to impairment, disability, and handicap are strongly culture-bound. It is unlikely that a universally acceptable classification of these determinant factors is achievable at present, for the same reasons that preclude a universally accepted classification of the determinants of health. Nevertheless, classifications of environmental factors may prove useful in the analysis of national situations and in the development of solutions at the national level.

The classifications developed in the area of mental health, whether for the entire population or for specific age groups, are based mainly on the ICD. The chapter on mental and behavioural disorders has been thoroughly updated in the Tenth Revision of the ICD, and the ICIDH will have to reflect these changes, as well as those embodied in other publications. The Council of Europe Committee of Experts has recently drawn up a report discussing the present use of the ICIDH in the study of mental retardation. Recognizing the ICIDH as an important step towards generally accepted criteria for legal definitions, the report of the United Nations Commission on Human Rights, mentioned earlier, encouraged WHO to revise the ICIDH, with special attention to the problems of impairments and disabilities related to mental health. Similar concerns apply to the problems of cognitive function often associated with aging. Publication of the French-language version of the ICIDH in 1988 evoked particular interest among psychiatrists; as WHO Collaborating Centre for the ICIDH, the *Centre technique national d'Etudes et de Recherches sur les Handicaps et les Inadaptations* (CTNERHI) is devoting an important part of its activities to the applications of the ICIDH and its relation to other classifications in mental health. As a result of these developments, the area of mental health will be treated with particular care in the revision of the ICIDH.

The revision process will also address detailed changes to items within the classification, and must take into account the improved understanding of basic biological mechanisms, particularly as regards impairments. In some cases this will have implications for preferred terminology and will entail changes to terms that have become obsolete.

The current version of the ICIDH contains definitions and examples that are highly culture-specific (e.g. references to "pouring tea") or that are inappropriately characterized according to sex; these will be corrected whenever possible. In addition, typographical and factual errors, and definitions no longer consistent with those in ICD–10 will be similarly remedied. A small number of these have been corrected in the present reprint.

An "umbrella" term is needed to encompass the spectrum of experiences linked to impairment, disability, and handicap: the term "disablement" has been suggested, but is not universally accepted. In some languages there appears to be no single suitable term. The official French-language version, for example, uses "handicap" as an umbrella term, stressing that it does not cover a monolithic reality, but is the result of different levels of experience; this version also uses a term signifying "disadvantage" for the third level of experience in the classification (as do the Italian, Japanese, and Portuguese versions). French-speaking Canadians, on the other hand, appear to prefer the word "handicap" for this third level and do not make use of an umbrella term. Agreement on the use of an existing term or on the introduction of a new term will require much thought and discussion during the revision of the ICIDH.

Training and presentation materials for the ICIDH have been developed, notably in France by CTNERHI, and in Quebec, Canada (as a video presentation). In addition, the *Real Patronato de Prevención y de Atención a Personas con Minusvalía* in Madrid has supported the development of a computer-based program in Spanish for its application. Identification and sharing of these and other experiences, and some standardization of approaches, will enhance their usefulness.

The revision of the ICIDH will be based upon a review of reports and documents describing its use, and consultation with expert representatives from relevant disciplines. The opinions of international and nongovernmental organizations, including organizations of people with disabilities, which deal with different aspects of disability will continue to be sought and considered throughout the process of revision, and representation of experiences from countries in the various Regions of WHO will be ensured.

INTRODUCTION

The ability-capability gap, the discrepancy between what health care systems can do and what they might do, constitutes one of the greatest challenges for those concerned with health care and welfare. The hope is widely shared that improvements in the availability of relevant information could make an important contribution to the development of policies more appropriate for the solution of these problems. Choices are being made all the time, even if only by default. It is assumed that the quality of choices would be enhanced if the degree to which decisions were related to information, a description of the situation as it is, was increased. The classification schemes in this manual are offered as frameworks to facilitate the provision of such information.

Information relevant to health experiences

The material incorporated in this manual is concerned with dimensions of health-related experience complementary to those embraced by the concept of disease. The manual is published by the World Health Organization, albeit only for trial purposes, in response to a resolution of the World Health Assembly. Inescapably, this carries with it the implication that information about these additional dimensions is useful and even necessary for health service planning. As the collection of this extra information can only increase the burden on existing information systems, it is prudent to begin by indicating why the need for it arises.

Routinely available data

The organization and planning of a health care system are generally based on information generated routinely from the system. This tends to be of two types. First, there are indicators of need, such as recorded morbidity experience. Second, there are data that are the by-products of administrative requirements; these consist of information on resource inputs, such as manpower or hospital beds, or derivatives from these such as waiting lists, and on resource utilization, such as patient loads in various sectors of the system.

All this information is the product of an existing health care system, and it is therefore subject to the same assumptions as those underlying available health care processes. In other words, questions of utility and relevance, as they concern the appropriateness both of the care system and of the information that derives from it, are difficult to examine. This means that the potential for fundamental appraisal or evaluation of the processes is very limited, and as a result alternative approaches may too readily be neglected.

If health care processes are to be evaluated, they must be goal-oriented, because the appraisal is concerned with the extent to which goals are attained. The prime requirement is for clearly specified outcome goals. This would permit study of the extent to which these outcome goals are met, the effectiveness of the particular health care process; the inputs necessary to attain this, the efficiency of the process; and its availability and uptake, the equality of its distribution. [1] Management is always likely to be processing data on resource provision and utilization but, as should be evident, these are relevant mainly to efficiency and equality goals. Although attempts have been made to evaluate effectiveness by these means, resource data can serve only as proxies for what is of real concern.

Data for evaluation

Three aspects are fundamental to any attempt to evaluate the effectiveness of health care processes. These are:
  i)   contacts made with the system;
  ii) how the system responds to contact; and
  iii) the outcome of contact.
Assessment of the second of these, how the system responds to contact, requires only brief consideration. In principle the means for structuring information relevant to this aspect are widely available. Thus resource data of the types already indicated can be used for global appraisals, whilst the newly developed International Classification of Procedures in Medicine [2] provides a framework for documenting specific responses by the system. However, the nature of information pertinent to the first and third aspects is less straightforward and therefore requires more detailed examination.

The outcome of contact has to be related to goals. In general, these have not been formulated with the precision necessary to permit evaluation. However, the simplest requirement of a health care system is that some beneficial change in the individual's situation or status should result from contact with the system. If no such change can be detected, then the value

1. Cochrane, A. L. (1972) *Effectiveness and efficiency: random reflections on health services.* London, Nuffield Provincial Hospitals Trust.

2. World Health Organization (1978) *International classification of procedures in medicine,* Geneva, vol. 1 and 2.

of a given health care process is seriously open to question. Thus, the challenge is to devise a means of describing the status of an individual in such a way that, by assessing status when contact is first made and then again after the system has responded, change can be recorded. This change would provide a measure of outcome.

Unfortunately, the nature of the challenge alters as the burden of morbidity changes. Thus when the major force of disease is expressed as acute illness, of which the acute infections provide the most notable example, simple and unequivocal measures are readily available from which outcome can be assessed. These consist of the occurrence or otherwise of the disease, and recovery or a fatal outcome. For this purpose, terms derived from the International Classification of Diseases (ICD) provide a valuable and relevant means for studying health experience, and the underlying cause concept is additionally helpful. Moreover, generalizations in population terms are simple to derive and are justifiable because disease control is so dependent on community-based action. Herein lay the nineteenth-century foundations of public health and of the value of indirect indicators of community health, such as perinatal mortality.

As the acute infections come under control, other diseases assume a greater importance. As long as the latter are life-threatening, the simple indicators, such as mortality, continue to be valuable, so that ICD terms retain their usefulness for evaluation. However, as technological power is developed, the situation changes. Conditions like diabetes and pernicious anaemia can be controlled even though their underlying causes cannot be eliminated. Mortality and even the occurrence of disease then have less relevance to evaluation other than that relating to primary prevention, and ICD terms no longer reflect outcome goals, particularly when the rules for assignment to categories are constrained by the underlying cause concept. Hence the need to identify manifestations, a facility made possible by options in the Ninth Revision of the ICD. This extension of the classification does permit evaluation, because of the potential for a manifestation to be abolished or suppressed; change after contact can thus be recorded. However, the extent to which population generalization can be developed on this basis remains to be explored further.

Diseases that are self-limiting or amenable to prevention or cure account for only part of the spectrum of morbidity. In fact, the very success of control measures for these diseases has resulted in the increasing importance of a residue of conditions that do not come into this category. These include the effects of trauma, impairments of special sense organs, mental retardation and mental illness, and the chronic diseases of middle and later life, particu-

larly heart disease, stroke, bronchitis, and arthritis. Disorders like these are
coming to dominate current morbidity experience in some countries and
they are especially noteworthy as causes of disability. For these disorders, a
manifestation code is very useful for identifying the calls that may be made
on different types of service, but it can only rarely serve as a means of
indicating change in the individual's status after contact with a health care
system.

Consequences of disease

The difficulties arise because of the limited scope of the medical model
of illness. The kernel of the situation is represented by the concept of disease,
which may be depicted symbolically as a sequence,

etiology ⟶ pathology ⟶ manifestation.

The ICD is based on this model, the components of the sequence being
variously and severally identified within the classification. However, such a
model fails to reflect the full range of problems that lead people to make
contact with a health care system. Some consideration of the nature of the
reasons for contact is therefore necessary.

Sickness interferes with the individual's ability to discharge those functions
and obligations that are expected of him. In other words, the sick person is
unable to sustain his accustomed social role and cannot maintain his customary relationships with others. This view is sufficiently broad to take account
of the vast majority of calls that are likely to be made on a health care
system. At one extreme, it embraces life-threatening disease, and, at the
other, it includes less medical experiences such as anxiety or the wish for
advice and counselling. The only class of contact not incorporated in this
approach is contacts made in the absence of illness phenomena, such as
attendances for prophylactic inoculation. Provision for certain of these non-
sickness-related contacts has been made ever since the Sixth Revision of the
ICD, and this aspect has now been tackled systematically in the Ninth
Revision (Supplementary Classification of Factors influencing Health
Status and Contact with Health Services – V Code).

Although, in everyday practice, the medical model of illness portrayed
above provides a very efficient approach to disorders that can be prevented
or cured – the impact of illness is relieved secondarily as the underlying
condition is brought under control – it is incomplete because it stops short
of the consequences of disease. It is the latter, particularly, that intrude
upon everyday life, and some framework is needed against which understanding of these experiences can be developed; this is especially true for

chronic and progressive or irreversible disorders.

The sequence underlying illness-related phenomena thus needs extension. This can be presented as

disease ————➤ impairment ————➤ disability ———➤ handicap

The nature of these different dimensions of the consequences of disease, their definition, and the basis for developing three separate classification schemes, will be considered in greater depth in the first section of this manual. At this juncture it is probably sufficient to note that the distinctions facilitate policy development in response to the problems, clarifying the potential contributions of medical services, rehabilitation facilities, and social welfare respectively. By the same token, the proposals offer different types of status descriptor, with a varying potential for change, so that the needs of evaluative studies are anticipated. Furthermore, the descriptors provide the basis for study of both the reasons why an individual makes contact with a health care system and a related problem, underutilization, where it is the determinants of why not all of those with a given health status make contact with the system that are of interest.

Development of the classifications

Many approaches have been made to measurement of the consequences of disease. One strand has been concerned to structure experience in clinical and rehabilitation contexts, and this has been particularly notable in the United States of America. Great emphasis has generally been placed on functions such as activities of daily living, and the approach has been based on assessment procedures.[3] A more recent development has sprung from demands for ascertainment of disabled individuals, either in prevalence surveys or for determining eligibility for pensions and other welfare provisions. The purpose has been to identify categories or groups of people fulfilling predetermined criteria; works of this type have therefore been concerned more with assignment than with assessment. However, the range of applications has been considerable, extending from routine health statistics and specific cash benefits to health service planning, social security, social administration, and social policy.

Those concerned with measurement on a community scale, by the gathering and presentation of statistical tabulations relevant to these purposes,

3. Wood, P. H. N. & Badley, E. M. (1978) An epidemiological appraisal of disablement. In: Bennett A. E., ed., *Recent advances in community medicine*, Edinburgh, Churchill Livingstone.

were stimulated by these activities. A preliminary scheme was developed by Mrs Esther Cahana, and submitted to WHO by Israel in 1972. Within a few months, a more comprehensive approach was suggested by the WHO Centre for the Classification of Diseases, in Paris, after discussions between the Head of the Centre, Dr Madeleine Guidevaux, and Professor André Grossiord of Hôpital Raymond Poincaré, Garches, France. These suggestions were based on two important principles: distinctions were made between impairments and their importance, i.e., their functional and social consequences, and these various aspects or axes of the data were classified separately on different fields of digits. In essence, this approach consisted of a number of distinct, albeit parallel, classifications. This contrasted with the traditions of the ICD, wherein multiple axes (etiology, anatomy, pathology, etc.) are integrated in a hierarchical system occupying only a single field of digits.

WHO therefore invited a consultant, Dr Philip Wood of Manchester, England, to explore the possibility of assimilating the Paris proposals into a scheme compatible with the principles underlying the structure of the ICD. For this purpose, it was intended to supplement a three-digit hierarchical classification of impairments, analogous in form to the ICD, by three additional digits dealing with disability and handicap in the form of mobility, physical dependence, and economic dependence. At the same time, preliminary attempts were made to systematize the terminology applied to disease consequences. These suggestions were circulated informally in 1973, and help was solicited particularly from groups with a special concern for rehabilitation.

It soon emerged that difficulties arose not only from nomenclature, but also from confusion about the underlying concepts. After clarification of these ideas, it became apparent that a single scheme conforming to the taxonomic principles of the ICD was unsatisfactory. Whilst impairments could be dealt with in this manner, a synthesis of the different dimensions of disadvantage could be accomplished only by making arbitrary and often contradictory compromises between the various dimensions or roles identified. The principle was therefore advanced that a classification of handicap had to be structured differently, based on ordination of the different states of each dimension. This development is discussed in greater detail in the first section of this manual.

After discussions with Professor Grossiord and the Paris centre, separate classifications of impairments and handicaps were prepared. These were circulated widely in 1974, and many comments and suggestions for improvement were received. Particularly helpful contributions to the development of these schemes have been made at various stages on behalf of the International Continence Society (Eric Glen), the International Council of Ophthalmology (August Colenbrander), the International and European Leagues against Rheumatism (Philip Wood), the International Society for Prosthetics and Orthotics (the late Hector W. Kay), and Rehabilitation International (K.-A. Jochheim). Acknowledgement must also be made to the individual contributions of Elizabeth M. Badley and Michael R. Bury, and to the work of Bernard Isaacs and Margaret Agerholm. Various memoranda were also made available by the World Health Organization, both at its headquarters in Geneva and at its Regional Office for Europe in Copenhagen.

Further discussions were then held, involving WHO and representatives of the International Social Security Association and the Social Security Department of the International Labour Office. Responsibility for collating comments and developing definitive proposals was undertaken by Dr Wood. These were submitted for consideration by the International Conference for the Ninth Revision of the International Classification of Diseases in October 1975. At this juncture the scheme incorporated a supplementary digit to identify disability, and the whole approach was acknowledged as being to a large extent experimental and exploratory. Having considered the classification, the Conference recommended its publication for trial purposes. In May 1976, the Twenty-ninth World Health Assembly took note of this recommendation and adopted resolution WHA 29.35, in which it approved the publication, for trial purposes, of the supplementary classification of impairments and handicaps as a supplement to, but not as an integral part of, the International Classification of Diseases.

The present manual, published under this authority, represents a considerable recasting of the detailed proposals submitted to the Ninth Revision Conference. The hierarchical arrangement of the impairment classification has been radically altered so as to allow for taxonomic spaces more closely related to importance and frequency of occurrence; a completely new disability classification has been introduced, resembling in structure the impairment classification; and the handicap classification has been augmented. These alterations have been carried out in the light of preliminary field testing, comments by the International Federation of Societies for Surgery of the Hand (Alfred B. Swanson), and further comments by the individuals and organizations noted previously and by UNESCO and OECD.

Practical application of the classifications
Scope and structure of the manual

The manual contains three distinct and independent classifications, each relating to a different plane of experience consequent upon disease.

(a) *Impairments* (I code), concerned with abnormalities of body structure
    and appearance and with organ or system function, resulting from
    any cause; in principle, impairments represent disturbances at the
    organ level.

(b) *Disabilities* (D code), reflecting the consequences of impairment in
    terms of functional performance and activity by the individual;
    disabilities thus represent disturbances at the level of the person.

These two are perhaps the least controversial. Their taxonomic structure
resembles that of the ICD in that they are hierarchical, with meaning
preserved even if the codes are used only in abbreviated form; also they are
exhaustive. The contrast between the I and D codes stems from the nature
of what is being classified. Impairments resemble disease terms in the ICD in
that they are best conceived of as threshold phenomena; for any particular
category, all that is involved is a judgement about whether the impairment is
present or not. On the other hand, disabilities reflect failures in accomplishments so that a gradation in performance is to be anticipated; provision has
thus been made for recording of the degree of disability, and also of future
outlook.

(c) *Handicaps* (H code), concerned with the disadvantages experienced
    by the individual as a result of impairments and disabilities; handicaps
    thus reflect interaction with and adaptation to the individual's
    surroundings.

**Handicap is more problematical. The structure of the Handicap classification
is radically different from all other ICD-related classifications. The items are not
classified according to individuals or their attributes but rather according to the
circumstances in which people with disabilities are likely to find themselves,
circumstances that can be expected to place such individuals at a disadvantage
in relation to their peers when viewed from the norms of society.** The scheme is
not exhaustive and is restricted to key social roles,what have been regarded as
the most important dimensions of disadvantageous experience – orientation,
physical independence, mobility, occupation, social integration, and economic
self-sufficiency. For each of these dimensions a gradation of circumstances is
possible, so that specification of the individual's status in regard to each is
required. These properties determine that the codes are not hierarchical in the
customarily accepted sense, and abbreviation is possible only by neglecting
certain of the dimensions. Perusal of the outline of the H code should indicate
these characteristics more clearly.

These and other features of the three classification schemes are examined
at greater length in the first section of the manual. Assessment and assignment to relevant categories are also discussed. In addition, the manual
includes an index to impairments.

Data sources

With the exception of surveys and research enquiries, the primary source for data of the type covered by this manual is the records of contacts made with a care system. It is therefore necessary to review what is entered in records, so that its suitability for classification according to the present schemes can be considered. Contact will be made with a caring professional, who may be a physician, a nurse, a remedial therapist, a social worker, or a pensions assessor, or who may be from various other health-related professions. The essence of the transaction that ensues is that the individual's problems are elicited and assessed. The conclusions of the assessment, augmented by some of the information exchanged, are likely to be noted in the case records.

The process may be exemplified by medical diagnosis. Symptoms and signs are elicited from the individual. These are then assessed and considered in conjunction. On the basis of known constellations of characteristics it is usually possible to assign the individual's problems to a predetermined group or category in the form of a specific diagnosis. Three aspects are especially noteworthy. First, the raw data are individual-oriented, the symptoms and signs present in one specific individual. In terms of an information system all that can be derived are enumerations of individuals with particular attributes. Second, meaning is given to these diverse attributes by categorization, identifying a basis for interrelationships between them. This generates group-oriented information, which has two important properties. There is a potential to make inferences about individuals in the group that go beyond the limits of data necessary for categorization; for instance, in addition to labelling the individual's collection of symptoms and signs an ideal diagnosis also indicates etiology, pathology, and prognosis. There is also a potential to aggregate category-oriented data on the basis of more general commonalities, such as the chapters of the ICD, and this enhances transmission of simplified information. The third significant aspect of medical diagnosis is that it provides a medium for communication between one professional and another, largely on the basis of the attributes that can be inferred from the category label.

On this foundation, it is possible to examine the nature of information likely to be available on disease consequences. A number of difficulties are immediately apparent, and their influence can most clearly be revealed by pursuing the analogy with medical diagnosis. First, objectives inevitably differ appreciably between the various professions; thus what is germane for a remedial therapist is unlikely to be so for a social worker. This variation in emphasis and concern introduces a lack of comparability into data. Second, heterogeneity tends to be exaggerated by the fact that in this context most professions are concerned mainly with assessment and its associated individual-oriented data, without there having been much standardization of procedures. Information of this type does not lend itself to simplification for transmission in an information system; consider, for instance, an enumeration of difficulties experienced in the activities of daily living, which is not particularly helpful either for service planning or for indicating policy options.

A third difficulty is that unifying concepts analogous to disease entities have not generally been developed. As a result few category-oriented data have been available, an important factor contributing to shortcomings in policy development and planning in regard to the disabled. Finally, the lack of appropriate concepts with transprofessional currency has led to communication difficulties, a problem compounded by ambiguity and confusion in terminology.

This manual does not presume to resolve all these difficulties, as its publication for trial purposes indicates. However, it is presented for exploration as a means of overcoming some of the problems. It seeks to contribute to the promotion of uniformity in broad concepts and terminology and, by indicating ways in which individual attributes may be grouped together for simplification, to encourage standardization and an improvement in the comparability of data. Today's case records are unlikely to contain all the necessary detail in a form suitable for rigorous application of the classification schemes. Nevertheless, it is hoped that the manual will have educational value, stimulating the collection and recording of more appropriate data.

Pending the gathering of more ideal information with these classification schemes specifically in mind, it is still possible to exploit the approach with existing records. Some indication of the possibilities may be helpful. The underlying cause of an individual's difficulties, the disease, can usually be ascertained from the diagnosis stated in medical records, so that ICD coding is not too difficult. In nonmedical records the underlying cause may not be easy to determine, but in these contexts it is usually likely to be of less importance in any case. In either type of record the more immediate consequences of disease, the major impairments, are likely to be noted, so that coding to the I code should also not present insuperable obstacles. The main aspect likely to command attention in the future relates to identification criteria and their relation to severity.

The D code calls for information that is also likely to be in the records already, although care will be necessary in regard to variation resulting from the use of clinical assessment, functional tests (including the activities of daily living), or questionnaires. The categories proposed should lend themselves to assessment and to elicitation by questionnaire without much difficulty. However, caution is also necessary in appreciating the manner in which disability may be established in different contexts — a professional medical definition based on a physician's judgement, a behavioural definition derived from performance of selected activities, or a legal definition framed in terms of eligibility for various benefits.

The assessment of handicap unavoidably includes consideration of the dimensions and categories included in the H code. Thus the basic assignment should not prove unduly difficult or give rise to any additional labour. This suggests that the scheme is feasible, but its comparability and validity will only be revealed by further experience. For retrospective application to existing records the major difficulty is likely to be incomplete information, but the orientation of whatever material may be available can still be instructive.[4] Nevertheless in applying the classification certain problems need to be borne in mind. First, disadvantage may be perceived in three different ways: subjectively, by the individual himself; by others who are significant to the individual; and by the community as a whole. Second, there is ambiguity over how to regard third-party handicap. Third, it is not possible for any scheme intended for international use to correspond exactly with eligibility for various benefits. These and related problems are examined in greater detail in the first section of the manual.

Uses of information

It is a fundamental principle of taxonomy that classification is subordinate to a purpose. This would appear to preclude the possibility of any general-purpose scheme and, as has been noted earlier, to embrace all the planes of disease consequences has necessitated three distinct taxonomies. However, this canon does not debar development of classifications that simultaneously are able to serve a number of purposes, as the durability and robustness of the basic structure of the ICD indicate; the price of such flexibility is no more than the occasional controversial compromise. The schemes presented in this manual have been developed with these considerations in mind, at the same time trying to take into account the needs of a wide variety of potential users, and it may be helpful if some of the uses are identified specifically.

The three major classes of needs are analogous to those for which the ICD is most widely used. These are:

---

4. Wood and Badley, *op.cit.*

(a) for the production of statistics on the consequences of disease. These are necessary for surveillance of trends, for service planning, and for research enquiries into the epidemiology and sociology of disability and handicap. For the latter purpose it is discordances in severity between the three planes and the determinants of these differences that are particularly instructive;

(b) for the collection of statistics relevant to the utilization of services. These not only provide the basis for service planning, but also facilitate evaluation;

(c) for indexing and case record retrieval according to the attributes identified in the classifications.

As has been noted, each of the three schemes is restricted to a single plane of the consequences of disease. This means that a full profile, extending from the underlying cause of the impairment to the disadvantage that ensues, can be derived only if all three codes are used in conjunction with the ICD so as to yield a complete specification of status. It is hoped that in everyday clinical contexts the full scheme will be utilized so that, in addition to fulfilling the above needs, it may be possible to promote more sensitive and comprehensive assessment of individual problems and to facilitate more critical evaluation.

In addition, though, the codes have been conceived so that they are capable of independent use for specific purposes. It is envisaged that for these more limited applications the orientation of the impairment, disability, and handicap codes will be, respectively, for medical, rehabilitation, and welfare services. However, disability and handicap data are also relevant to broader areas of social policy, such as those concerned with education, employment, and housing. Finally, it is also hoped that the codes may contribute to standardization in problem identification and record-keeping among different professional groups.

Although there have been demands for a means of classifying impairments and disabilities in conjunction with the ICD, the nature and scale of the schemes proposed go considerably further than many persons had originally envisaged. This is in keeping with the World Health Organization's declared goal of "Health for all by 2000". Better information on the consequences of chronic and disabling conditions should make an essential contribution to the realization of this aim.

The development of these classification schemes has covered much new ground. Indebtedness to the work of many individuals and groups has already been acknowledged. Nevertheless, experience in this area of classification, especially in the practical applications, is extremely limited. After extensive consultation, it seemed that the most constructive plan to secure overall coherence and consistency in these tentative and experimental proposals would require that their final integration and editing be undertaken by a single individual. The more usual process of revision by group deliberation would best be exploited when variations in practical experience from widespread field application were to hand, and when conflicting views needed resolution. For these reasons users encountering difficulties in the application of the classifications are asked to communicate their comments to:

Strengthening of Epidemiological and Statistical Services,
World Health Organization,
1211 Geneva 27,
Switzerland.

The following ICD abbreviations and conventions have been used in this manual:

NEC not elsewhere classified

NOS not otherwise specified

* combination category (for reduction of information on a number of impairments to a single category)

other in the titles of categories in the classification, the term "other" indicates any specification not included in preceding categories (for example, inclusion in the category "complete deficiency, right" requires that the right side be specified; the next category is "other complete deficiency", and to this would be assigned those where the left side or both sides were specified, and also those where the side affected was not specified)

decimal digits 8 and 9 used for "other" and "unspecified" categories, respectively

SECTION 1

THE CONSEQUENCES OF DISEASE

The response to illness
    Acute and chronic illness

A unifying framework
    Planes of experience
    Impairment
    Disability
    Handicap
    Integration of concepts

Application of the concepts
    Terminology
    Deviation from norms
    Measurement
    Classification of impairments
    Classification of disabilities
    Dimensions of disadvantage
    Classification of handicaps

THE CONSEQUENCES OF DISEASE

This manual is concerned with improving information on the consequences of disease. Such an endeavour is dependent on appreciation of the nature of health-related experiences. It is necessary, therefore, to begin with an attempt to clarify these.

The response to illness

In contemplating illness phenomena it is customary to invoke the concept of disease. This notion and its derivatives, such as the International Classification of Diseases (ICD), consider pathological phenomena as though they were unrelated to the individuals in whom they occur. Long-prevalent traditions in thought have fostered such separation, tending to make categorical distinctions between the natural and human worlds, between non-living and living, and between body and mind. However, certain limitations in this approach are evident. By isolating thoughts of disease from consideration of the sufferer, the consequences tend to be neglected. These consequences — responses by the individual himself and by those to whom he relates or upon whom he depends — assume greater importance as the burden of illness alters. The problems may be illustrated by contrast between acute and chronic processes.

Acute and chronic illness

In colloquial speech, "acute" tends to indicate something sharp or intense, whereas "chronic" implies severity in terms of being objectionable or very bad. For this reason patients can be alarmed when they learn that the official nomenclature for their condition includes the latter term — e.g., chronic bronchitis. However, professional usage of the words remains closer to their etymology. Thus "acute" means "ending in a sharp point", implying a finite duration, which, classically, culminates in a crisis. On the other hand "chronic", which is derived from a word meaning "time", indicates "long-continued". A host of interrelated properties is associated with these contrasts in time scale, and these render unnecessary any precise formulation of the temporal boundary between acute and chronic processes.

The characteristics of acute illness may be exemplified by acute infections. Onset of the condition is frequently sudden. There may be almost total prostration, not least because rest is commonly regarded as facilitating recovery. Furthermore, there is the prospect of a limited period in this state. These three features help to promote two important responses. First, suspension of everyday obligations comes about in such a way as to be acceptable both to the sufferer and to others. Secondly, the situation encourages unquestioning capitulation to professional advice. For the health professional the situation is also relatively straightforward. The interval between exposure to the putative dominant cause and development of the illness tends to be short, so that simple models of causality can account for disease occurrence. The high incidence of many acute conditions provides the professional with experience of a diversity of responses. Uncomplicated decisions are called for; either action is imperative or there is time for reflexion on what form of support might be appropriate. Most acute illnesses are self-limiting; some may be life-threatening, but the remainder, because of their finite duration, pose a minimal threat to the patient. These features encourage a paternalistic attitude by the professional, so that symptom relief is regarded largely as a means of tiding the patient over until the crisis has passed. Finally, the concentration of effort needed to treat acute conditions is not too difficult to justify; although primary prevention may offer a more economical solution, commitment of resources for secondary control by health services is at least time-limited. Thus, in policy terms, the options in regard to what can be accommodated within a given level of health service investment tend to be clear-cut, the choices being concerned with whether various acute health problems should be responded to at all.

Chronic illness presents different challenges. The onset is usually insidious; there may be a gradual progression of symptoms, or more permanent problems may develop as the sequel to a number of acute episodes. Confidence and hopes are undermined; the experience is usually difficult to account for, no end is in sight, and self-perception — the sense of identity — is assaulted by changes in the body and its functional performance. Activity restriction, though at times severe, nevertheless usually falls short of total incapacity until very late in the course of the illness. Legitimation or acceptance by others can be more difficult when a degree of independent existence is possible, not least because obligations cannot be suspended indefinitely; some way of coming to terms with the altered situation therefore becomes necessary. Finally, the persistence of problems implicitly reveals limitations in the potency of medical treatment, so that professional advice is often accepted with less assurance. The health professional is confronted with complementary difficulties. The prevalence of chronic conditions may be high, but their incidence is relatively low; common experience therefore relates more to the range of problems unfolding in a limited number of patients. This has been one of the forces contributing to the development of medical specialization and the concentration of care in large institutions such as hospitals. Clinical decisions themselves are more problematic, the insidious progress of chronic disease making diagnosis more difficult; definitive conclusions often have to be deferred, yet action may be called for in the face of this uncertainty.

Demands differ in other important aspects. Thus, the impact of the condition on the individual, though important, does not dominate the scene to the exclusion of all else. Clinical status has to be set against the background of life, moving, as it does, between home and work. Symptoms reflecting impairments and disabilities call for attempts at amelioration in their own right. Sensitivity is also taxed; virtually everyone experiences acute illness at some time, so that it is not too difficult to project oneself into the situation of the patient, but personal knowledge of chronic suffering is much less widespread. Finally, the multidimensional quality of problems encountered in people with chronic illness tends to promote needs-based appraisals, which carry with them potentially inflationary consequences for health and welfare services. Thus policy formulation is more difficult and more controversial; it is necessary to choose which to respond to from the diversity of problems presented by affected individuals.

A unifying framework

The challenges for health care change as chronic illness comes to occupy a more dominant position. The sufferers themselves, the health professionals concerned to help them, and the policy makers and planners seeking to adapt to the different needs that arise — each in his different way encounters difficulties in coming to terms with the consequences of disease. The confusion that all three groups share stems largely from the lack of a coherent scheme or conceptual framework against which to set such experiences. These limitations in understanding are an obstacle to improving relevant information, and this in turn inhibits progress towards more helpful responses.

Planes of experience

The principal events in the development of illness are as follows:

(i) *Something abnormal occurs within the individual;* this may be present at birth or acquired later. A chain of causal circumstances, the "etiology", gives rise to changes in the structure or functioning of the body, the "pathology". Pathological changes may or may not make themselves evident; when they do they are described as "manifestations", which, in medical parlance, are usually distinguished as "symptoms and signs". These features are the components of the medical model of disease, as indicated in the Introduction.

(ii) *Someone becomes aware of such an occurrence;* in other words, the pathological state is exteriorized. Most often the individual himself becomes aware of disease manifestations, usually referred to as "clinical disease". However, it is also necessary to encompass two other types of experience.

(a) Not infrequently, symptoms may develop that cannot currently be linked to any underlying disease process. Something is certainly being exteriorized, even if it cannot be accounted for. Most health professionals would attribute such symptoms to a disturbance — as yet unidentified — of some essential structure or process within the body

(b) In contrast, some deviation may be identified of which the "patient" himself is unaware. Such pathology without symptoms sometimes constitutes subclinical disease, which is encountered with increasing frequency as screening programmes are extended. Alternatively, a relative or someone else may draw attention to disease manifestations

In behavioural terms, the individual has become or been made aware that he is unhealthy. His illness heralds recognition of *impairments,* abnormalities of body structure and appearance, and of organ or system function, resulting from any cause. Impairments represent disturbances at the organ level.

(iii) *The performance or behaviour of the individual may be altered* as a result of this awareness, either consequentially or cognitively. Common activities may become restricted, and in this way the experience is objectified. Also relevant are psychological responses to the presence of disease, part of so-called illness behaviour, and sickness phenomena, the patterning of illness manifested as behaviour by the individual in response to the expectations others have of him when he is ill. These experiences represent *disabilities,* which reflect the consequences of impairments in terms of functional performance and activity by the individual. Disabilities represent disturbances at the level of the person.

(iv) *Either the awareness itself, or the altered behaviour or performance to which this gives rise,* may place the individual at a disadvantage relative to others, thus socializing the experience. This plane reflects the response of society to the individual's experience, be this expressed in attitudes, such as the engendering of stigma, or in behaviour, which may include specific instruments such as legislation. These experiences represent *handicap,* the disadvantages resulting from impairment and disability. The explicit concern with the value attached to an individual's performance or status obviously makes this the most problematical plane of disease consequences.

Each of the last three planes in this sequence — exteriorization, objectification, and socialization — now requires more detailed consideration. This will be followed by further examination of the interrelationships between the underlying concepts, supported by examples to highlight the distinctions.

Impairment

> *In the context of health experience, an impairment is any loss or abnormality of psychological, physiological, or anatomical structure or function*

Two aspects of this definition need to be stressed. First, the term "impairment" is more inclusive than "disorder" in that it also covers losses; e.g., the loss of a leg is an impairment, but not a disorder. Secondly, in reaching agreement on terminology with other international agencies, it has been necessary to make certain modifications to the definitions included in a preliminary draft of this manual.[1] In the draft, functional limitations were regarded as being elements of disability, whereas they have now been assimilated with impairments; this alteration helps to resolve boundary distinctions that originally lacked clarity.

Impairment represents deviation from some norm in the individual's biomedical status, and definition of its constituents is undertaken primarily by those qualified to judge physical and mental functioning according to generally accepted standards. Impairment is characterized by losses or abnormalities that may be temporary or permanent, and it includes the existence or occurrence of an anomaly, defect, or loss in a limb, organ, tissue, or other structure of the body, or a defect in a functional system or mechanism of the body, including the systems of mental function. Being concerned to describe identity at a particular point in time, impairment is neutral in regard to a number of associated features, and this needs to be stressed. Thus impairment is not contingent upon etiology, how the state arose or developed; both ascribed and achieved status, such as genetic abnormality or the consequences of a road traffic accident, are included. Use of the term "impairment" does not necessarily indicate that disease is present or that the individual should be regarded as sick. Equally, the deviation from the norm does not need to be perceived by the impaired individual, as should be clear from what has been said above about exteriorization. On the same grounds, a concept of latent impairment constitutes a contradiction in terms — the individual exposed to or harbouring an extraneous etiological agent of disease is not impaired; impairment ensues only when the agent has initiated a reaction by the body so that pathological processes develop.

---

1.   Wood, P.H.N. (1975) *Classification of impairments and handicaps* (Unpublished document WHO/ICD9/REV. CONF/75.15)

Disability   *In the context of health experience, a disability is any restriction or lack (resulting from an impairment) of ability to perform an activity in the manner or within the range considered normal for a human being*

In providing the link between impairment and handicap, it is fairly easy for the concept of disability to appear somewhat vague, variable, or arbitrary. As already noted, however, functional limitation is now regarded as an aspect of impairment, and this should resolve most of the difficulties. Impairment is concerned with individual functions of the parts of the body; as such it tends to be a somewhat idealistic notion, reflecting potential in absolute terms. Disability, on the other hand, is concerned with compound or integrated activities expected of the person or of the body as a whole, such as are represented by tasks, skills, and behaviours.

Disability represents a departure from the norm in terms of performance of the individual, as opposed to that of the organ or mechanism. The concept is characterized by excesses or deficiencies of customarily expected behaviour or activity, and these may be temporary or permanent, reversible or irreversible, and progressive or regressive. The key feature relates to objectification. This is the process through which a functional limitation expresses itself as a reality in everyday life, the problem being made objective because the activities of the body are interfered with. In other words, disability takes form as the individual becomes aware of a change in his identity. Customary expectations embrace integrated functioning in physical, psychological, and social terms, and it is unrealistic to expect a neat separation between medical and social aspects of activity. For instance, physical incapacities and socially deviant behaviours equally transgress what is expected of the individual – the important differences between them concern the value that is attached to such deviations, and any sanctions that may be applied as a result; such valuations relate to the concept of handicap, rather that to that of disability.

In attempting to apply the concept of disability, there is a need for caution in how the ideas are expressed. By concentrating on activities, disability is concerned with what happens – the practical – in a relatively neutral way, rather than with the absolute or ideal and any judgements that may attach thereto. To say that someone *has a disability* is to preserve neutrality, nuances of interpretation in regard to his potential still being possible. However, statements phrased in terms of being rather than having tend to be more categorical and disadvantageous. Thus to say that someone *is disabled,* as if this were an adequate description of that individual, is to risk being dismissive and invoking stigma.

Handicap

> *In the context of health experience, a handicap is a disadvantage for a given individual, resulting from an impairment or a disability, that limits or prevents the fulfilment of a role that is normal (depending on age, sex, and social and cultural factors) for that individual*

Three important features of this concept should be borne in mind:

(i) some value is attached to departure from a structural, functional, or performance norm, either by the individual himself or by his peers in a group to which he relates;

(ii) the valuation is dependent on cultural norms, so that a person may be handicapped in one group and not in another – time, place, status, and role are all contributory;

(iii) in the first instance, the valuation is usually to the disadvantage of the affected individual.

The state of being handicapped is relative to other people – hence the importance of existing societal values, which, in turn, are influenced by the institutional arrangements of society. Thus, the attitudes and responses of the non-handicapped play a central role in modelling the ego concept, and defining the possibilities, of an individual who is potentially handicapped – the latter has a very limited freedom to determine or modify his own reality. In this context it is relevant to take note of differences in societal responses to visible as opposed to invisible impairments, and to serious as opposed to trivial disadvantages.

Handicap is characterized by a discordance between the individual's performance or status and the expectations of the particular group of which he is a member. Disadvantage accrues as a result of his being unable to conform to the norms of his universe. Handicap is thus a social phenomenon, representing the social and environmental consequences for the individual stemming from the presence of impairments and disabilities. The essence of an adverse valuation by society is discrimination by other people, but the concept is, nevertheless, essentially neutral as regards its origins. Thus the individual's own intention is of no immediate concern; disadvantage can arise when the individual deviates in spite of his own wishes, but it can also develop when the deviation is inadvertent or the product of his own choice. The concept also assimilates phenomena such as invalidism or excessive dependence upon an institution.

Integration of concepts

The ideas just discussed can be linked in the following manner:

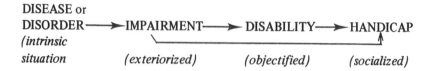

DISEASE or
DISORDER ——►IMPAIRMENT ———► DISABILITY——►HANDICAP
(intrinsic
situation   *(exteriorized)*   *(objectified)*   *(socialized)*

Although this graphic representation suggests a simple linear progression along the full sequence, the situation is in fact more complex. In the first place, handicap may result from impairment without the mediation of a state of disability. A disfigurement may give rise to interference with the normal operation of cues in social intercourse, and it may thus constitute a very real disadvantage, to say nothing of the embarrassment that the disfigured individual may feel. In this example, though, it would be difficult to identify any disability mediating between the disfigurement and the disadvantage. Similarly, a child with coeliac disease, who is functionally limited, may be able to live a fairly normal life and not suffer activity restriction; he could nevertheless suffer disadvantage by virtue of his inability to partake of a normal diet. More important than these incomplete sequences is the possibility of interruption at any stage. Thus one can be impaired without being disabled, and disabled without being handicapped. The corollary of this is that there can be striking disparities in the degree to which the various elements of the sequence depart from their respective norms, and, as a result, one cannot assume consonance in degrees of disability and handicap. For instance, one individual with rheumatoid arthritis may be only mildly disabled and yet at a severe disadvantage, whereas another person with the same disease who is much more severely disabled may, perhaps because of greater support from the family or social network, experience considerably less disadvantage.

Further complexity is introduced by two other phenomena. First, certain disabilities can retard or conceal the development or recognition of other abilities; thus, an impairment of language can interfere with the expression of other and dependent qualities, such as intelligence. Secondly, there can be a variable degree of influence in a reverse direction along the sequence. Thus, the experience of certain handicaps can engender, as part of illness behaviour, not only various disabilities but at times even the impairment of certain faculties; as already noted, each of the concepts is largely independent of its origins, so that these secondary phenomena should not be excluded.

The great value of presenting the concepts in this way is that a problem-solving sequence is portrayed, intervention at the level of one element having the potential to modify succeeding elements. This is especially relevant to the purposes of this manual, since the sequence is also valuable as a means of identifying information deficits. It will probably be helpful to present further examples of how the concepts are expressed.

– A child born with a finger-nail missing has a malformation – a structural impairment – but this does not in any way interfere with the function of the hand and so there is no disability; the impairment is not particularly evident, and so disadvantage or handicap would be unlikely.

– A myope or a diabetic individual suffers a functional impairment but, because this can be corrected or abolished by aids, appliances, or drugs, he would not necessarily be disabled; however, the non-disabled juvenile diabetic could still be handicapped if the disadvantage is considerable, e.g., by not being allowed to partake of confectionery with his peers or by having to give himself regular injections.

– An individual with red-green colour blindness has an impairment, but it would be unlikely to lead to activity restriction; whether the impairment constitutes a handicap would depend on circumstances – if his occupation were agricultural he might well be unaware of his impairment, but he would be at a disadvantage if he aspired to drive a railway engine, because he would be prevented from following this occupation.

– Subnormality of intelligence is an impairment, but it may not lead to appreciable activity restriction; factors other than the impairment may determine the handicap because the disadvantage may be minimal if the individual lives in a remote rural community, whereas it could be severe in the child of university graduates living in a large city, of whom more might be expected. (This example illustrates how any attempt to differentiate between intrinsic and extrinsic components of handicap in fact neglects the fundamental property of this concept, which expresses the resultant of interaction between the intrinsic and the extrinsic; the intrinsic aspect is identified by any impairments and disabilities that may be present.)

– Perhaps the most graphic example of someone who is handicapped without being disabled is the individual who has recovered from an acute psychotic episode but who bears the stigma of being a "mental patient"; note that this handicap complies with the definition, because it is consequent upon impairment and disability, but that neither the impairment nor the disability exists at the time the handicap develops.

– Finally, the same handicap can arise in different situations, and therefore as a result of different disabilities. Thus, personal hygiene might be difficult to maintain, but its antecedents could be very different for someone accustomed to a washbasin as compared with a way of life where ablutions are performed in a lake, or in a fast-moving river, or yet again in a desert environment.

Application of the concepts

Before one can attempt to apply this conceptual framework for the consequences of disease, it is necessary to deal with two related difficulties.

Terminology

A major reason for the lack of information about the disabled in society is that the various agencies concerned have not shared a common unambiguous definition of what constitutes disablement, impairment, and limitation.[2] Incongruence in problem identification also occurs, as was highlighted in a review of the need for definitions: "The word disability refers to an abnormality which interferes with function to a significant degree. A complete diagnosis should describe the disability, the abnormality underlying it, and the cause of the abnormality. Parents tend to think in terms of disability, whereas doctors often speak of abnormalities or their causes, and this may lead to misunderstanding."[3] Most of the terms over which confusion arises have been used with common-sense meanings in everyday speech and writing. The underlying problem has been that concepts relating to disability and disadvantage have been insufficiently explored, and, as a result, no systematized language usage specific to these concerns has developed.

Two initiatives by the World Health Organization have helped to transform this state of affairs. The first took place in 1975-1976, when approval in principle was given to the conceptual framework put forward in the preliminary draft of this manual. The second, built on this foundation over the succeeding years, has secured agreement on usage for the most important terms between a number of international agencies. This preferred nomenclature has been employed throughout.

Although too much can be made of the importance of semantic distinctions, the acid-test for a preferred nomenclature is whether it promotes practical benefits. The latter should come about as a clearer description of processes reveals to what extent and in what way problems may be solved. Considerable care has been applied to the selection of descriptive terms in this manual, so as to reinforce the conceptual distinctions. This effort can be seen at two levels:
(i) Avoidance of the same word to identify an impairment, a disability, and a handicap. In colloquial speech there has been a trend to euphemism, with words being debased as mental retardation first became mental disability and then mental handicap. This succeeds only in blurring the distinctions; the disadvantage experienced by individuals with psychological impairments can vary, so that it is inappropriate to refer to a handicap as "mental". Thus the descriptive adjectives "mental" and "physical" may correctly be applied to impairments, but their use in relation to disabilities is loose and to handicaps quite unsuitable. It is perhaps vain to hope that the tide of careless usage can be reversed, but at least in serious discourse the logic of terminology

2.   Townsend, P. (1967) *The disabled in society*. London, Greater London Association for the Disabled.

3.   Mitchell, R. G. (1973) Editorial. *Develop. Med. Child. Neurol.*, 15, 279-280.

should be exploited to reinforce the conceptual framework.

(ii) In addition to seeking different descriptive terms, the use of different parts of speech also seemed to be appropriate. Thus for the qualities represented by impairments an adjective derived from a substantive is apposite, but for the activities included as disabilities a participle was deemed more suitable, the "-ing" ending emphasizing the dynamic aspect. An exhaustive consistency in this regard has not been possible, but a trend should be apparent.

These points can best be illustrated with examples:

Impairment	Disability	Handicap
language	speaking ⎤	
hearing	listening ⎬	orientation
vision	seeing ⎦	
skeletal	⎧ dressing, feeding	physical independence
	⎩ walking	mobility
psychological	behaving	social integration

For specific impairments, the nomenclature and classification preferred by relevant international organizations, such as the International Society for Prosthetics and Orthotics, have been employed wherever possible.

Deviation from norms

All three of the concepts relevant to the consequences of disease — impairment, disability, and handicap — depend on deviations from norms. The amount of deviation regarded as being present depends on the operation of a definition of the norm in question, be the specification implicit or identified. There are three approaches to such definition:

(i) For quantitative phenomena, such as body height, the exploitation of statistical concepts of "the normal" and of deviations therefrom is of some help. However, although the approach may be useful in indicating conformity to type, there are limitations and certainly statistical methods can have little application when the norm relates to a value. The attraction of statistical concepts is that they appear to be value-free, which appeals to the many health professionals with a scientific background. Such striving for objectivity is encouraged by the illusion that common notions of causality in science are non-normative, as if they represented matter-of-fact relations or contingent connexions between events. The reality is that the very notion of what will count as a causal agent in disease is connected with a normative view of the normal or healthy organism.

(ii) Normative views, such as those just indicated, are determined by reference to some ideal. This approach to the norm implicitly relates to threshold phenomena. To some degree the situation may be circumscribed by enunciation of standardized criteria for assignment to the class of those conforming, or failing to conform, to the ideal. Such methods can be applied to unquantified phenomena in the domain of impairment, and to most disabilities.

(iii) Drawing further on the theory of deviance, yet other norms are determined by social responses. These are relevant to some disabilities and to most handicaps. In general, these norms are more difficult to categorize reproducibly, other than by recourse to cumbersome and highly arbitrary methods such as those used for determining eligibility for benefits. However, the particular relevance of social norms in the present context is that they indicate that an individual's perceptions — his belief that he has a problem — or the identity that other people attribute to the individual can both give rise to disadvantage.

Another problem stems from the very nature of norms. Specific individual impairments or disadvantages are not themselves universal, although when they are taken in aggregate most of us fail to escape some departure from the norm. The social definition of problems allows one to resolve the difficulties, because value orientation relates to social interest; thus, in a social context, disease occurring in wild species is likely to be of little concern, whereas maladies affecting domestic animals are of greater interest. Departures from the norm thus need to be regarded in such a way that views are tempered by consideration of the feasibility and desirability of intervention to restore the norm. This is also the place to introduce another note of caution. There has been a recent vogue for promoting the notion of social handicap, drawing attention to such problems as poverty and poor housing out of relation to their direct influences on health. While one has sympathy with any attempt to combat social deprivation, such dilution of the concept of handicap is unhelpful because it tends to confound identification of specific health-related experiences and the means by which these might be controlled.

Measurement

In order to measure the consequences of disease, those who are affected have to be ascertained. The process of ascertainment of the disabled and handicapped is itself somewhat dubious, at least as an absolute proposition, and two crucial questions have to be acknowledged. The first concerns the sense in which the individual is disabled or handicapped. This should have been made clear by the definitions of concepts, and it is hoped that the ideas will serve to rebut those who try to dismiss the scheme as an attempt to classify the unclassifiable. The second question, which underpins the first, is directed at the reason for ascertainment, because any attempt to clarify thinking in this area can be vulnerable to the protests of those who are concerned that categorization or labelling engenders stigma. However, this attitude surely denies the possibility of any coherent attempt to alter the present situation; until categories can be identified, one is unable to begin to count, and until counting is possible one cannot know how big the problems are or deploy the resources intelligently in an endeavour to control the problems.

In order to overcome the difficulties, it has been necessary to develop three separate classification schemes supplementary to the ICD — one concerned with each of the three principal concepts. These classifications are intended to facilitate study of some of the consequences of disease. They have been designed as coding systems that will allow details from individual case records to be reduced to standardized numerical form. This will allow the simplest form of measurement, by counting the numbers in each category. In turn, these counts can then be grouped with related problems so as to promote simplification for the preparation of statistical tabulations of aggregated data. The classifications therefore exemplify the underlying conceptual framework, but to a considerable degree their value can be considered separately from that of the theoretical constructs. This means that the classifications should be evaluated in the same way as the ICD — i.e., do they assist in the derivation of information of value to users?

Brief guidance on the acquisition of data compatible with these classifications was offered in the Introduction, and further suggestions about assessment and assignment have been made at the end of each of the succeeding chapters. However, it is now necessary to provide a more detailed description of the principles underlying the development of each of the three classifications.

Classification of impairments

For many clinicians, thought on an impairment axis is likely to be unfamiliar because it is cross-disciplinary. In many ways there is an approximate inverse relationship between the ICD and the impairment (I) code. Thus where the ICD allows a considerable array of causes, such as those for cardiovascular and respiratory diseases, the I code makes relatively limited provisions because the functional consequences of these various conditions are much more limited. Similarly, the functional consequences of an amputation are virtually identical, be it due to trauma or to a congenital deficiency, and so only a single series of coding categories is provided; the ICD would have to be used to distinguish which cause applied. However, amputations also illustrate how parts of the ICD fail to provide sufficient detail for clinical management, a problem that applies to other disorders of the limbs as well. An attempt has been made to embrace the diversity of the functional consequences of these conditions in some detail, although this has necessitated recourse to a fourth digit.

The basic structure of the I code consists of two digits supplemented by a decimal digit; as just noted, in some parts the use of a fourth digit has been suggested as well. An attempt has been made to allot taxonomic space in relation to the frequency and importance of the various types of impairment. In form the code resembles the ICD, in that it is hierarchical and meaning is preserved even if the code is used only in abbreviated form. Again, like disease terms in the ICD, impairments are best conceived of as threshold phenomena; for any particular category, all that is involved is a judgement about whether the impairment is present or not. In developing a single exhaustive code, it has been necessary to make compromises in specificity and taxonomic purity for the sake of simplicity, and a number of aspects obviously could not be accommodated; perhaps the most important omissions are individual composite functions such as jumping and creeping. The classification had to simplify details, and the overwhelming consideration has been to identify the most important feature influencing the intervention or support the individual might be likely to need. As soon as multiple impairments are present, specificity becomes less important. However, to allow for specificity when it is desired, an option has been provided wherever possible; each individual impairment may be coded (multiple coding) or special combination categories, identified by an asterisk, may be used instead if the information has to be reduced to a single category. Alternatively, the code could be used to identify the most limiting impairment. This would be by analogy with the underlying cause concept in relation to the ICD. In this connexion, the prime function of the level of detail offered is to define the content of classes. It is up to the user to determine how much detail is recorded, so that the situation resembles that with the ICD — definition of subclasses by specification of considerable detail, but tabulation of aggregated data by broader classes such as ICD chapters.

One other problem is that some categories of the I code and of the ICD appear to overlap. This occurs particularly in regard to symptoms, but a review of the purposes of the two classifications is likely to settle the difficulty. Interest in the condition leading to the consumption of medical services would probably require an ICD statement. A study of the reasons why people make contact with a health care system could use either I code or ICD statements, depending on the terms of reference of the study. Evaluation of the effectiveness of a health care system would call for two I code statements – one indicating initial status, and the other the status after contact with the system. Perhaps the likeliest use of the I code, though, would be as an indicator of unmet needs. In these circumstances, one might well wish to restrict consideration to relatively persistent impairments, eliminating transitory states and other trivia by adopting duration and severity criteria – such as that I code statements should be recorded only for impairments that had been present for a specified period of time, or that had persisted after medical treatment. Finally, it can be seen that in many ways a classification of impairments may be regarded as a classification of health-related problems that individuals are likely to encounter. The I code therefore has relevance to problem-oriented record systems and may be of value to those interested in automating the processing of such records, short of introducing full interactive visual display with a computer.

Classification of disabilities

In the preliminary draft of this manual a limited scheme was put forward for recording disability in a rather arbitrary manner, by means of a digit supplementary to the I code. This proved to be inadequate for many purposes. As a result, a more comprehensive disability (D) code has been designed – one that encompasses the more important behaviours and activities associated with everyday life. The key influence in designing this classification has been the feasibility of recording the interface between the individual and his environment in such a way as to display his potential; this may be supplemented by the handicap classification as a means of indicating the extent to which potential is realized. Perhaps the ideal aim for the D code would be to present a profile of the individual's functional abilities, as determined from what disabilities were present, in such a way that reciprocal specification of the environment allowed matching with the individual's capabilities. For instance, in the context of job placement, a factory extending over two floors but with toilet facilities located on only one of these would require separate specification of each floor for purposes of matching with the (residual) functional abilities of potential employees. If this effort succeeded, the D code could then be used as a means of screening that could be applied not only to job placement in vocational rehabilitation but also to school placement, rehousing the disabled, identifying vulnerability in the elderly, and other related purposes.

In view of these considerations, it proved necessary to eliminate much of the complexity and detail present in conventional assessments, such as those of the activities of daily living. Only in this way could procedures be developed that would be simple and confined to the most basic or key functions. The actual assessment procedures may need to retain their complexity but, as in the I code, this additional detail could be incorporated in the D code more as a means of clarifying the content of broader classes. In the circumstances, it is understandable that the D code is less developed than the schemes for impairment and handicap. However, its form allows of expansion in response to additional needs uncovered by further field experience. The basic structure of the code consists of two digits, with the option of a supplementary decimal digit, but even the nine main chapters have not been fully utilized so far. Once again, the taxonomic form resembles that of the ICD in being hierarchical, meaning being preserved even if the code is used only in abbreviated form – this feature is essential for facilitating matching of the individual and environmental circumstances. However, there is one important difference from both the ICD and the I code – disabilities are not threshold phenomena; they reflect failures in accomplishments, so that a gradation in performance is to be expected. Provision has therefore been made for recording the degree of disability by means of a supplementary digit. Furthermore, those engaged in rehabilitation also find a judgement on future outlook of potential value, and so provision has also been made for this on an additional supplementary digit.

Dimensions of disadvantage

Before proceeding to the classification of handicaps, it is necessary to consider further the nature of disadvantage. Any direct attempt to measure values is fraught with difficulties. However, one can identify certain fundamental accomplishments that are related to the existence and survival of man as a social being and are expected of the individual in virtually every culture. An individual with reduced competence in any of these dimensions of existence is, *ipso facto*, disadvantaged in relation to his peers. The degree of disadvantage attached to reduced competence may vary appreciably in divers cultures, but some adverse valuation is almost universal. The key accomplishments include the ability of the individual to:

(i) orient himself in regard to his surroundings, and to respond to these inputs;

(ii) maintain an effective independent existence in regard to the more immediate physical needs of his body, including feeding and personal hygiene;

(iii) move around effectively in his environment;

(iv) occupy time in a fashion customary to his sex, age, and culture, including following an occupation (such as tilling the soil, running a household, or bringing up children) or carrying out physical activities such as play and recreation;

(v) participate in and maintain social relationships with others;

(vi) sustain socioeconomic activity and independence by virtue of labour or exploitation of material possessions, such as natural resources, livestock, or crops.

These six dimensions may be designated as survival roles, and the handicap classification is based on this analysis. However, before describing this scheme, a number of other points have to be taken into account.

The only value assumed in this analysis is that existence and survival are necessary and good. In a consideration of health-related problems this proposition would not appear to require justification. Survival roles have the merit of being broadly transcultural; in fact, disturbance of orientation, physical dependence, immobility, restricted occupation, social isolation, and poverty are the biggest and most frequent problems of the impaired and disabled, even in urbanized and industrialized societies with appreciable surplus wealth. Survival roles by no means exhaust the dimensions of handicap, and cognizance must be taken of other disadvantages. Maslow's hierarchy of needs [4] would appear to present a useful conceptual framework for understanding these problems. The three lowest planes are physiological, safety, and social needs, and it is with these that the handicap classification deals, largely in that order. Ego needs and status recognition come next, and the highest level is self-fulfilment. Maslow then asserts that man is motivated to satisfy needs in a predetermined order; the individual is no longer driven once a need is satisfied, but higher needs will be ignored until more basic needs are met. These hierarchical distinctions can be of value in helping to determine priorities. Certainly the dominance of survival roles emerges very clearly from such an analysis. Moreover, the symbolic values attached to such basic functions as eating and excretion can be seen to reflect a higher level of need. However, these higher needs are more difficult to measure, and there is little to commend directing attention to more difficult problems as long as basic needs are neglected. For this reason the classification makes little provision for disadvantage other than in relation to survival roles. Those interested in studying these aspects in greater detail will doubtless develop their own supplementary schemes.

---

4.   Maslow, A.H. (1954) *Motivation and personality*. New York, Harper & Row.

One important source of confusion needs to be disposed of at this stage. Disadvantage has frequently been equated with dependence. Certainly dependence has the advantage of being fairly easy to define, and therefore to measure. Moreover, a fundamental self-sufficiency in regard to physical and material accomplishments is important, not least because dependence on others entails making demands on their productivity and time. This aspect is complicated in many societies, in which changes in family size, geographical mobility, and obligations within the family have led to demands for dependence to be responded to collectively rather than individually — a problem compounded by demographic changes that increase the proportion of the population at greatest risk, the elderly. The principal obstacle to subsuming disadvantage within the term "dependence" is that it obscures social needs that can themselves, if met, go a long way to overcoming many of the disadvantages associated with irremediable physiological and safety needs. Underlying this is the fact that the notable feature of highly integrated societies is the extreme dependence of the individual on others, both for social relationships and for opportunities for occupation and economic self-sufficiency. The reality is that man is a social being; the social relations an individual enjoys are equally as essential for his survival as is competence in attending to physiological needs. Thus man's situation can more appropriately be described as one of interdependence. Moreover, this helps to highlight another important aspect — if disadvantage in one dimension is reduced, disadvantage in another may also be made more bearable.

The apparent lack of a clear operational differentiation has obviously served to perpetuate confusion between disability and handicap. In the past, the means of identifying handicap usually depended on the ascertainment of disability and its severity. To infer the existence of disadvantage from the presence of certain disabilities may not appear unreasonable, but important assumptions both about values and about the interrelationship between disadvantage and the nature and severity of disability are implied by this approach. Thus there is a danger that the goal of social action may too readily become deflected to disability alone. This is a reductionist response, submerging handicap within disability, and it can encourage views that are insensitive to other dimensions of disadvantage, so that inequities result. These are exemplified by the common and yet unacceptable differences in the financial recompense offered to the disabled according to the cause of their impairment, feelings of guilt presumably accounting for the preferential rates often given to those disabled at war. There is also a tendency to concentrate excessively on disability resulting from physical impairments, to the neglect of that consequent upon psychological impairments.

The difficulty is that the measure too readily determines the activity. For instance, measurements of intelligence quotients (IQ) have tended to influence educational opportunities out of relation to need, educational potential, or anything other than the availability of buildings and institutions to cope with the categories so identified. Much the same has happened with disability. Administratively, it may appear to be simpler to institute ascertainment and control at the level of disability; certainly one can see the need for some yardstick to reconcile the frequently conflicting needs of society and of the individual. However, disability will only indirectly influence disadvantage, and it is therefore important to be quite clear about one's goals. If handicap is the prime area of social concern, not all those with activity restriction are necessarily at a disadvantage — because activity restriction cannot be viewed as a sociological phenomenon *per se*. There is a distinct cleavage between disability and handicap, both conceptually and in the means for intervention, and methodological obstacles need not compel social action on disadvantage to be determined by measures of disability alone. As evidence for this, the handicap classification is provided as the means of studying disadvantage direct.

Classification of handicaps

Having indicated the challenge, it is now necessary to explain why the handicap (H) code takes the form that it does. An attempt to classify nominal variables is relatively easy. The principal requirement is that the classification should be exhaustive. In medical contexts, the other requirement of simple logic — that the classes be exclusive — is more problematical, since more than one disease, impairment, or disability can occur in the same individual. The difficulty can be overcome, however, either with multiple coding or by adopting conventions such as combination categories or assignment rules based on concepts such as the underlying cause. A hierarchy can be imposed on a classification of nominal variables by identifying similarities and grouping these together. An example is provided by the various axes of the ICD, based on etiology, system, location, and nature. Impairments and disabilities can be classified in a similar manner.

The essential property of nominal variables is that the classes are mutually exclusive. When one turns to the concept of handicap, the situation is very different. Whereas manifestations are finite, consequences relate to a more complex whole that is difficult to partition. In terms of disadvantage, the consequences are that an individual is unable to sustain the roles to which he is accustomed or to attain those to which he might otherwise aspire. Through these roles one can identify dimensions or components of disadvantage, but these interact in such a way that it is important to reflect them all, while keeping them distinct. Thus the first task in constructing a taxonomy of handicap is to identify the dimensions that one wishes to classify. This has been undertaken in the preceding section, where it was acknowledged that values, being difficult to measure, may best be studied in an indirect manner. Thus the H code classifies items not according to individuals or their attributes, but according to the circumstances in which disabled people are likely to find themselves – circumstances that can be expected to place such individuals at a disadvantage in relation to their peers when judged by societal norms. It is then necessary to recognize that one is concerned with degrees of these dimensions; thus, for each dimension, a gradation of circumstances is possible, and a specification of the individual's status in regard to each is therefore required. As a result, the code is not hierarchical in the customarily accepted sense, and abbreviation is possible only by arbitrarily neglecting certain of the dimensions – rather than by compromise between various roles or axes, as is incorporated in the ICD. Similarly, an attempt at synthesis would be both presumptuous and self-defeating; it would involve the imposition of value judgements in a dangerously subjective realm.

Perusal of the outline of the H code should indicate these characteristics more clearly, when it will be seen that, as a descriptor, an H code statement is a means of summarizing the situation semi-quantitatively, rather than identifying discrete categories. Overlap between categories in the different dimensions has been kept to a minimum, but it could not be eliminated altogether. Thus an individual who is bedfast is not only immobile, but also totally dependent on others for care. Theoretically it might be possible to eliminate such overlap, but in practice it appeared preferable for each dimension to stand on its own, for the reasons noted above. Much thought has been given to the ordination, the partitioning of the states of the various dimensions. Not only must categories be meaningful in themselves, but differentiation between them must be feasible by fairly simple and yet reliable means. For these reasons a full spectrum of sensitivity, spanning the available nine digits, has not always been possible. One must acknowledge here the value of concepts such as that of critical interval needs,[5] which has been incorporated in the physical independence dimension and is much superior to more arbitrary distinctions such as those based upon the duration for which help is needed. How successful all these attempts have been, and how appropriate the ordination within each dimension is, will become apparent only after further practical trials of the classification.

5.   Isaacs, B., & Neville, Y. (1975) *The measurement of need in old people.* (Scottish Health Service Studies, No. 34) Edinburgh, Her Majesty's Stationery Office.

Certain other problems are likely to be encountered. First, disadvantage may be perceived in three different ways — subjectively, by the individual himself; by others who are significant to the individual; and by the community as a whole. Secondly, there is ambiguity over how to regard third-party handicap — i.e., handicap in an individual who is not himself impaired but who suffers disadvantage because of the demands made upon him by chronic illness or disability in the family. The difficulty is that, in following the definition of handicap with rigour, it is not possible to take account of such people in the present context, since their disadvantage is not consequent upon their own impairment and disability. Thirdly, it should be obvious from what has been said that it is not possible for any scheme intended for international use to correspond exactly with eligibility status for various benefits.

SECTION 2

CLASSIFICATION OF IMPAIRMENTS

IMPAIRMENT

Definition   In the context of health experience, an impairment is any loss or abnormality of psychological, physiological, or anatomical structure or function

(Note : "Impairment" is more inclusive than "disorder" in that it covers losses — e.g., the loss of a leg is an impairment, but not a disorder)

Characteristics   Impairment is characterized by losses or abnormalities that may be temporary or permanent, and that include the existence or occurrence of an anomaly, defect, or loss in a limb, organ, tissue, or other structure of the body, including the systems of mental function. Impairment represents exteriorization of a pathological state, and in principle it reflects disturbances at the level of the organ

LIST OF TWO-DIGIT CATEGORIES OF IMPAIRMENT

1   INTELLECTUAL IMPAIRMENTS

Impairments of intelligence (10-14)

10	Profound mental retardation
11	Severe mental retardation
12	Moderate mental retardation
13	Other mental retardation
14	Other impairment of intelligence

Impairments of memory (15-16)

15	Amnesia
16	Other impairment of memory

Impairments of thinking (17-18)

17	Impairment of flow and form of thought processes
18	Impairment of thought content

Other intellectual impairments (19)

19	Other intellectual impairment

2   OTHER PSYCHOLOGICAL IMPAIRMENTS

Impairments of consciousness and wakefulness (20-22)

20	Impairment of clarity of consciousness and of the quality of conscious experience
21	Intermittent impairment of consciousness
22	Other impairment of consciousness and wakefulness

Impairments of perception and attention (23-24)

23	Impairment of perception
24	Impairment of attention

Impairments of emotive and volitional functions (25-28)

25 Impairment of drives

26 Impairment of emotion, affect, and mood

27 Impairment of volition

28 Impairment of psychomotor functions

Behaviour pattern impairments (29)

29 Impairment of behaviour pattern

3 **LANGUAGE IMPAIRMENTS**

Impairments of language functions (30-34)

30 Severe impairment of communication

31 Impairment of language comprehension and use

32 Impairment of extralinguistic and sublinguistic functions

33 Impairment of other linguistic functions

34 Other impairment of learning

Impairments of speech (35-39)

35 Impairment of voice production

36 Other impairment of voice function

37 Impairment of speech form

38 Impairment of speech content

39 Other impairment of speech

4 **AURAL IMPAIRMENTS**

Impairments of auditory sensitivity (40-45)

40 Total or profound impairment of development of hearing

41 Profound bilateral hearing loss

42 Profound hearing impairment in one ear with moderately severe impairment of the other ear

43 Moderately severe bilateral hearing impairment

44 Profound hearing impairment in one ear with moderate or lesser impairment of the other ear

45 Other impairment of auditory sensitivity

Other auditory and aural impairments (46-49)

46   Impairment of speech discrimination
47   Other impairment of auditory function
48   Impairment of vestibular and balance function
49   Other impairment of aural function

5   OCULAR IMPAIRMENTS

Impairments of visual acuity (50-55)

50   Absence of eye
51   Profound visual impairment of both eyes
52   Profound visual impairment of one eye with low vision in the other eye
53   Moderate visual impairment of both eyes
54   Profound visual impairment of one eye
55   Other impairment of visual acuity

Other visual and ocular impairments (56-58)

56   Visual field impairment
57   Other visual impairment
58   Other ocular impairment

6   VISCERAL IMPAIRMENTS

Impairments of internal organs (60-66)

60   Mechanical and motor impairment of internal organs
61   Impairment of cardiorespiratory function
62   Impairment of gastrointestinal function
63   Impairment of urinary function
64   Impairment of reproductive function
65   Deficiency of internal organs
66   Other impairment of internal organs

Impairments of other special functions (67-69)

67   Impairment of sexual organs
68   Impairment of mastication and swallowing
69   Impairment related to olfaction and other special functions

7   **SKELETAL IMPAIRMENTS**

Impairments of head and trunk regions (70)

70   Impairment of head and trunk regions

Mechanical and motor impairments of limbs (71-74)

71   Mechanical impairment of limb
72   Spastic paralysis of more than one limb
73   Other paralysis of limb
74   Other motor impairment of limb

Deficiencies of limbs (75-79)

75   Transverse deficiency of proximal parts of limb
76   Transverse deficiency of distal parts of limb
77   Longitudinal deficiency of proximal parts of upper limb
78   Longitudinal deficiency of proximal parts of lower limb
79   Longitudinal deficiency of distal parts of limb

8   **DISFIGURING IMPAIRMENTS**

Disfigurements of head and trunk regions (80-83)

80   Deficiency in head region
81   Structural deformity in head and trunk regions
82   Other disfigurement of head
83   Other disfigurement of trunk

Disfigurements of limbs (84-87)

84   Failure of differentiation of parts
85   Other congenital malformation
86   Other structural disfigurement
87   Other disfigurement

Other disfiguring impairments (88-89)

88   Abnormal orifice
89   Other disfiguring impairment

9   GENERALIZED, SENSORY, AND OTHER IMPAIRMENTS

Generalized impairments (90-94)

90   Multiple impairment
91   Severe impairment of continence
92   Undue susceptibility to trauma
93   Metabolic impairment
94   Other generalized impairment

Sensory impairments (95-98)

95   Sensory impairment of head
96   Sensory impairment of trunk
97   Sensory impairment of upper limb
98   Other sensory impairment

Other impairments (99)

99   Other impairment

1 INTELLECTUAL IMPAIRMENTS

Intellectual impairments include those of intelligence, memory, and thought
   Excludes : impairments of language and learning (30-34)

IMPAIRMENTS OF INTELLIGENCE (10-14)

   Includes : disturbances of the rate and degree of development of
      cognitive functions, such as perception, attention,
      memory, and thinking, and their deterioration as a
      result of pathological processes

10 **Profound mental retardation**
   IQ under 20
   Individuals who may respond to skill training in the use of legs,hands,
   and jaws

11 **Severe mental retardation**
   IQ 20-34
   Individuals who can profit from systematic habit training

12 **Moderate mental retardation**
   IQ 35-49
   Individuals who can learn simple communication, elementary health
   and safety habits, and simple manual skills, but do not progress in
   functional reading or arithmetic

13 **Other mental retardation**

13.0   *Mild mental retardation*
   IQ 50-70
   Individuals who can acquire practical skills and functional reading and
   arithmetic abilities with special education, and who can be guided towards social conformity

13.8   *Other*

13.9   *Unspecified*

14 **Other impairment of intelligence**

14.0   *Global dementia*
   Dementia affecting all cognitive functions and skills
   Includes : deterioration of cognitive functioning as a result of cerebral
         disease or trauma

14.1   *Lacunar or patchy dementia*
   With partial preservation of some cognitive functions and skills

14.2   *Other and unspecified dementia*
14.3   *Loss of learned skills*
14.8   *Other*
14.9   *Unspecified*

IMPAIRMENTS OF MEMORY (15-16)

15   **Amnesia**
Includes : partial or complete loss of memory for past events, and inability to register, retain, or retrieve new information
15.0   *Retrograde amnesia*
Impaired memory for happenings prior to some well-identified event
15.1   *Impairment of long-term memory*
15.2   *Impairment of recent memory*
Includes : congrade amnesia, impaired ability to acquire new information
15.3   *Psychogenic amnesia*
Irregularity of pattern of memory loss
15.4   *Impairment of memory for shapes*
15.5   *Impairment of memory for words*
15.6   *Impairment of memory for figures*
15.8   *Other*
15.9   *Unspecified*

16   **Other impairment of memory**

Memory includes the capacity to register, retain, and reproduce information
Includes : false memories and distortions of memory content
16.0   *Confabulation*
16.1   *Memory illusions*
Paramnesia
16.2   *Cryptomnesia*
Recall of facts or events without recognizing them as memories
16.3   *Other distortion of memory content*
16.4   *Forgetfulness*
16.8   *Other*
16.9   *Unspecified*

IMPAIRMENTS OF THINKING (17-18)

17   **Impairment of flow and form of thought processes**
Includes : disturbances affecting the speed and organization of
thought processes, and the ability to form logical
sequences of ideas

17.0   *Impairment of conceptualization or abstraction*
Relates to the ability to interpret the meaning of what is perceived,
to integrate perceptions, to form meaningful relations among perceptions, and to abstract

17.1   *Impairment of logical thinking*
Relates to the ability to relate ideas hierarchically

17.2   *Slowness of thought*

17.3   *Acceleration of thought*

17.4   *Perseveration*
Includes : "getting stuck", repeating phrases, and
constantly returning to same topic

17.5   *Circumstantial thinking*

17.6   *Obsessional ideas*

17.7   *Flight of ideas*
Includes : association of words by sound or rhyme

17.8   *Other*
Includes : incoherence of thought processes

17.9   *Unspecified*

18   **Impairment of thought content**
Includes : restriction of thought content, excessive or unrealistic
emphasis on and preoccupation with a particular set of
ideas to the exclusion of critical examination of the
ideas, and false beliefs not amenable to correction
through logical argument and reality testing

18.0   *Poverty of thought content*

18.1   *Overvalued ideas*

18.2   *Paranoid delusions*
A delusion is a false belief, impervious to the force of reason,
and not shared by others of similar education and cultural background. A paranoid delusion or idea of reference is a delusion
in which the individual considers that things in his surroundings
are happening especially in connexion with him

18.3   *Depressive delusions*
        Includes : delusions of guilt and impoverishment
18.4   *Delusional jealousy*
18.5   *Delusions of grandeur*
18.6   *Fantastic delusions*
18.7   *Hypochondriacal and nihilistic delusions*
18.8   *Other delusions*
18.9   *Other and unspecified*

OTHER INTELLECTUAL IMPAIRMENTS (19)

19   Other intellectual impairment

        Includes : Impairments of gnosis and praxis functions, where there is
                   disturbance of higher cortical functions underlying the
                   recognition and purposeful manipulation of objects

19.0   *Agnosia*
        Disturbed ability to recognise objects in the absence of impairments
        of consciousness, memory, and thinking
19.1   *Apraxia*
        Disturbed ability to perform learned purposeful movements in the
        absence of impairments of consciousness, memory, thinking, and
        motor capacity
19.2   *Acalculia*
        Disturbed ability to count and operate with numbers in the absence
        of impairments of consciousness, memory, and thinking
19.3   *Impairment of openness to new ideas*
19.4   *Misinterpretation*
        A misinterpretation is a false construction put by the individual on
        an occurrence
19.8   *Other*
19.9   *Unspecified*

Psychological impairments have been interpreted so as to include interference with the basic functions constituting mental life. For the purposes of this scheme, the functions listed as being impaired are those that normally indicate the presence of basic neurophysiological and psychological mechanisms. The level of organization of these functions is that usually recorded in a clinical examination of the central nervous system and in the examination of "mental status". In addition, some more complex psychological functions to do with drives, emotional control, and reality testing have also been included.

Conventionally symptoms such as hallucinations and delusions are usually thought of as very closely related to what have been defined here as impairments. In terms of the classification they can be regarded as the result of impairment of some essential psychological processes, which must normally exist even though we are as yet largely ignorant of their nature. For instance, severe anxiety symptoms can be thought of as an impairment of autonomic response control mechanisms; the same applies to morbid depressive affect, and to hypomanic affect. Similarly, hallucinations presumably result from impairment of mechanisms differentiating between self and non-self, while delusions indicate impairment of analogous mechanisms concerned with reality testing. For the purposes of the classification, symptoms have been included among impairments with the understanding that there is an inferred impairment of some underlying complex psychological mechanism.

Interferences with behaviour that represent complex purposeful and integrated sequences of interaction with and response to the environment and other persons are, for this purpose, properly regarded as disabilities rather than impairments.

IMPAIRMENTS OF CONSCIOUSNESS AND WAKEFULNESS (20-22)

20   **Impairment of clarity of consciousness and the quality of conscious experience**
Includes : various degrees of diminished wakefulness, and states characterized by changes in the level of wakefulness combined with altered awareness of self and the surrounding world
Excludes : Intermittent impairment of consciousness (21)

20.0   *Unconsciousness*
       Includes : coma, sopor, and stupor
20.1   *Clouding of consciousness*
       Includes : transitional syndrome or post-concussional state
20.2   *Narrowing of field of consciousness*
       Includes : when due to affect
20.3   *Delirium*
       Includes : twilight states
20.4   *Other confusional state*
       Includes : disorientation for time, place, and persons
20.5   *Dissociative state*
20.6   *Trance-like state*
       Includes : hypnotic state
20.7   *Akinetic mutism*
20.8   *Other*
20.9   *Unspecified*

21   Intermittent impairment of consciousness

       Includes : intermittent ictal disturbances characterized by a total or
                  partial loss of consciousness or by states of altered aware-
                  ness, and a variety of local cerebral signs and symptoms
21.0   *Profound intermittent interruption of consciousness*
       Includes : epilepsy with frequency of seizures of once per day or
                  greater
21.1   *Severe intermittent interruption of consciousness*
       Includes : epilepsy with frequency of seizures of once per week or
                  greater
21.2   *Moderate intermittent interruption of consciousness*
       Includes : epilepsy with frequency of seizures of once per month
                  or greater
21.3   *Mild intermittent interruption of consciousness*
       Includes : epilepsy with frequency of seizures less than once per
                  month
21.4   *Intermittent disturbance of consciousness*
       Includes : psychomotor epilepsy
21.5   *Other seizures*
       Includes : petit mal
21.6   *Other intermittent interruption of consciousness*
       Includes : syncope and drop-attacks
21.7   *Fugue states*

21.8   *Other*
21.9   *Unspecified*

22   Other impairment of consciousness and wakefulness
          Includes : impairments of the sleep/wakefulness cycle, both disturb-
                    ances affecting the quantity, quality, and pattern of the
                    processes of sleep and wakefulness,and impairments of
                    autonomic control of bodily functions that are influenced
                    by the sleep cycle

22.0   *Difficulty in getting off to sleep*
22.1   *Premature awakening from sleep*
          Includes : insomnia NOS
22.2   *Hypersomnia*
          Excessive sleeping
22.3   *Other impairment of sleep/wakefulness pattern*
          Includes : narcolepsy
22.4   *Enuresis nocturna*
22.5   *Other abnormality of acitivity during sleep*
          Includes : sleep-walking and sleep-talking
22.6   *Other impairm ent of sleep/wakefulness cycle*
22.7   *Sleepiness*
          Includes : somnolence
22.8   *Other*
          Includes : impairment of awareness (which is an undifferentiated
                    response to stimulus)
22.9   *Unspecified*

          IMPAIRMENTS OF PERCEPTION AND ATTENTION (23-24)

          Includes : disturbances of the functions enabling an individual to
                    receive through the senses, to process information about
                    the individual's own body and his environment, and to
                    focus selectively on aspects or parts of such information

23   Impairment of perception

23.0   *Impairment of the intensity of perception*
          Includes : changes in the degree to which qualities and attributes of
                    objects are perceived as vivid and impressing on the mind
          23.00   Uniform dulling of perception

23.01	Selective dulling of perception
	Includes : dulling in specific modalities
23.02	Uniform heightening of perception
23.03	Selective heightening of perception
	Includes : hypersensitivity to noise
23.08	Other
23.09	Unspecified

23.1   *Distortion of perception*

Includes : illusions,disturbed percepts where the objective content of sense data received in different modalities is distorted — something actually to be seen or heard is experienced as something else

Excludes : depersonalization (23.30)

23.10	Optical illusions
23.11	Acoustic illusions
23.12	Tactile illusions
23.13	Kinaesthetic illusions
23.14	Illusions in other sense modalities
23.15	Composite illusions
	Includes : pareidolic imagery
23.18	Other
23.19	Unspecified

23.2   *False perception*

Includes : hallucinations and pseudohallucinations, false or abnormal percepts that are not based on objective sense data

23.20	Visual hallucinations
23.21	Auditory hallucinations
23.22	Tactile hallucinations
23.23	Olfactory hallucinations
23.24	Gustatory hallucinations
23.25	Other hallucinations
23.26	Pseudohallucinations
	Includes : those in any sense modality
23.27	Oneiroid or dream-like hallucinatory state
23.28	Other
23.29	Unspecified

23.3   *Disturbance of body awareness*

23.30   Depersonalization

Experiences of alienation from one's own body, and the experience that one's relationship to the environment and surroundings (and vice versa) is altered

23.31   Derealization

Alteration of the feeling of reality/unreality and familiarity/unfamiliarity accompanying the perception of objects

Includes : déjà vu, jamais vu, and déjà vécu experiences

23.32   Body image disorder

Includes : phantom limb experiences

23.38   Other

23.39   Unspecified

23.4   *Disturbances of time and space perception*

Includes : time-standing-still, micropsy, and macropsy experiences

23.5   *Impairment of reality testing*

Includes : loss of ability to distinguish fantasy from reality

23.8   *Other*

23.9   *Unspecified*

24   **Impairment of attention**

Includes : disturbances of the intensity, span, and mobility of attention, the latter being a differentiated response to specific stimulus

24.0   *Distractibility*

24.1   *Impaired concentration*

24.2   *Narrowing of attention span*

24.3   *Impaired ability to shift focus of attention*

Includes : fixed attention

24.4   *Blank spells*

Includes : sudden stoppage or inattention while speaking for a few seconds or longer (may be due to thought-blocking or hallucination)

24.5   *Inattentiveness*

24.6   *Impairment of alertness*

Includes : diminished ability to stay alert as reflected by facial expression, speech, or posture

24.8   *Other*

24.9   *Unspecified*

IMPAIRMENTS OF EMOTIVE AND VOLITIONAL FUNCTIONS (25-28)

Refer to functions which contribute predispositions to action and purposeful behaviour

25   Impairment of drives

Includes : increase, decrease, or changes of pattern of various behaviours related to basic physiological needs or instincts

Excludes : impairment of volition (27)

25.0   *Decreased appetite*

Includes : anorexia

25.1   *Increased appetite*

Includes : hyperorexia and bulimia

25.2   *Impairment of sexual role*

Includes : lack of interest in a sexual relationship or contact

25.3   *Decrease of libido*

Includes : loss of libido

25.4   *Other impairment of sexual performance*

In the presence of normal libido

Includes : other disturbances of sexual functioning

Excludes : impairment of reproductive function (64) and of sexual organs (67)

    25.40   Impotence

    25.41   Ejaculatio praecox

    25.42   Frigidity

    25.48   Other

    25.49   Unspecified

25.5   *Alcohol dependence*

Includes : alcoholism

25.6   *Other drug dependence*

Includes : drug addiction

25.7   *Other pathological craving*

Includes : states of pathological craving related to substance dependence, and alcohol abuse

25.8 *Other*

25.80 Inability to sustain goals

25.81 Impairment of motivation

25.88 Other

25.9 *Unspecified*

26 Impairment of emotion, affect, and mood

Includes : disturbances of the intensity and quality of feelings and their somatic accompaniments, and disturbances of the duration and stability of feeling states

Excludes : pathological affect leading to narrowing of field of consciousness (20.2)

26.0 *Anxiety*

Includes : tense, worried look or posture, fearful apprehensive look, frightened tone of voice, and tremor

Excludes : tremor NOS (74.92)

26.00 Pathological anxiety

Includes : free-floating anxiety

26.01 Phobic anxiety

Includes : panic attacks

26.08 Other

26.09 Unspecified

26.1 *Depression*

Includes : anhedonia, and features such as sad, mournful look, tears, gloomy tone of voice, deep sighing, and choking of voice on depressing topic

26.2 *Other blunting of affect*

Includes : apathy, expressionless face or voice, uniform blunting whatever the topic of conversation, indifference to distressing topics, and flatness of affect

26.3 *Gross excitement*

Includes : the individual is manic, or throws things, runs or jumps around, waves arms wildly, shouts, or screams

26.4 *Other excitement*

Includes : euphoria, elation, hypomania, and unduly cheerful or smiling.

Excludes : psychomotor excitement (28.2)

26.5   *Irritability*

Includes :   angry outbursts

26.6   *Emotional lability*

Includes :   lability of one mood, changing from one mood to
another, and proneness to periods of depression or
elation

26.7   *Incongruity of affect*

Includes :   emotion shown but not congruent with topic, and
ambivalent affect

26.8   *Other*

26.80   "Catastrophic reaction"

26.81   Attempted control of affect display

Includes : attempt to suppress crying or anger, or to
fake a socially appropriate affect

26.82   Restlessness

26.83   Feelings of guilt

26.84   Emotional immaturity

26.85   Distress NEC

26.88   Other

26.9   *Unspecified*

Includes :   emotionally disturbed NOS, emotional impairment NEC

27   Impairment of volition

Includes :   disturbances of the capacity for purposeful behaviour
and control of own actions

Excludes :   obsessional traits (29.5) and mutism (30.0)

27.0   *Lack of initiative*

Includes :   impairment of manifestations of independent or un-
prompted action and self determination (the latter
including expression of personal opinion such as
spontaneous criticism or disagreement (not negativism, 27.3), situation-relevant acts such as closing
a door or lifting an object from the floor, asking
questions, and making requests or demands)

27.1   *Restriction of interests*

Includes :   loss of interests

27.2   *Overcompliance*

Includes :   excessive cooperation with elements of passivity,
and automatic submission

27.3   *Negativism*

27.4   *Ambitendence*

27.5   *Compulsions*
        Includes : rituals

27.6   *Impairment of impulse control*
        Includes : impulsive acts

27.8   *Other*
        Includes : impairment of adaptability, and other impairment
        of cooperation (e.g., misleading responses such as
        consistently negative responses and frequent self-
        contradiction, or appearance of being deliberately
        misleading)
        Excludes : Fatigability (28.5)

27.9   *Unspecified*

28   **Impairment of psychomotor functions**
        Includes : disturbances in the speed, rate, and quality of voluntary
        movements in the presence of an intact neural motor
        apparatus
        Excludes : involuntary movements of face (70.21), head (70.31),
        and body (70.54), and facial mannerisms (70.22)

28.0   *Slowness*
        Includes : slowness of psychic tempo, reduction of rate or speed
        of voluntary movements, and delays in responding to
        questions or in initiating requested tasks or movements
        (such as walking abnormally slowly, delay in perform-
        ing movements, slowness of speech with long pauses
        before answering or between words, and reduction of
        facial movements)
        Excludes : indistinct speech (35.5)

28.1   *Other underactivity*
        Includes : hypoactivity, semistuporous states, and reduction of
        extent of voluntary movements (such as sitting abnor-
        mally still, near total lack of voluntary movement,
        "doing nothing", and immobility of face)
        Excludes : stupor (20.0)

28.2   *Psychomotor excitement*

28.3   *Hyperkinesia in children*

28.4   *Other overactivity*
        Includes : over-talkativeness, pacing up and down restlessly, and
        not sitting down for a minute

28.5   *Fatigability*
Fatigue out of proportion to demands experienced
Includes : abnormal fall-off in alertness or speed of response or
              initiative
Excludes : sleepiness (22.7) and generalized fatigue (94.6)

28.8   *Other*

28.9   *Unspecified*

BEHAVIOUR PATTERN IMPAIRMENTS (29)

Refer to habitual patterns of behaviour that may interfere with social
adjustment and functioning. Such patterns of behaviour may be
present since adolescence and throughout most of adult life (e.g., in
personality disorders), or may occur as persisting sequelae of neurological or mental illnesses. They manifest themselves mainly as
accentuated character traits
Excludes : emotional lability (26.6)

29   Impairment of behaviour pattern

29.0   *Suspiciousness*

29.1   *Social withdrawal*
Includes : active avoidance of verbal or non-verbal interaction with
              other people, or of being in the physical presence of other
              people (e.g., avoidance of customarily expected social
              activities outside the home such as visiting kin or friends,
              going out with friends, and participating in games)

29.2   *Excessive shyness*
Includes : excessive sensitivity and vulnerability, and other impair-
              ment of ability to mix with people

29.3   *Hypochondriasis*

29.4   *Worrying*
Excludes : anxiety (26.0)

29.5   *Obsessional traits*
Includes : insecurity, indecisiveness, and repetition compulsion

29.6   *Other phobias*
Includes : agoraphobia

29.7   *Hostility*
Includes : aggressivity, being uncooperative, angry, overtly hostile.
              discontented, antagonistic, threatening, or violent
              (hitting out at or attacking others)

29.8   *Other*

    29.80   Histrionic traits

    29.81   Perplexity

           Includes : puzzlement

    29.82   Self-injury

           Includes : head banging, picking at sores, and beating eyes

    29.83   Other destructiveness

           Includes : damaging furniture and tearing up pages, maga-
                     zines, or clothing

    29.84   Attention-seeking

           Includes : will not leave (other) adults

    29.85   Solitary behaviour

    29.88   Other

29.9   *Unspecified*

    Includes : personality disorder NEC

3   LANGUAGE IMPAIRMENTS

Language impairments relate to the comprehension and use of language and its associated functions, including learning

IMPAIRMENTS OF LANGUAGE FUNCTIONS (30-34)

30   **Severe impairment of communication**

30.0   *Severe functional impairment of communication*
Includes : mutism

30.1   *Combined central disorders of speech and visual function with severe impairment of communication*
Includes : autism

30.2   *Impairment of higher centres for speech with inability to communicate*
Includes : severe dysphasia

30.3   *Other dysphasia*

30.4   *Other severe impairment of communication due to cerebral damage*

30.5   *Other total or severe interference with communication*

30.8   *Other impairment of higher centres for speech*

30.9   *Unspecified*

31   **Impairment of language comprehension and use**

31.0   *Central disorders of visual function with inability to communicate*
Includes : severe dyslexia

31.1   *Other dyslexia*

31.2   *Other central disorders of visual function*

31.3   *Impairment of vocabulary*

31.4   *Impairment of syntax*

31.5   *Impairment of semantic function*

31.8   *Other*

31.9   *Unspecified*

32   **Impairment of extralinguistic and sublinguistic functions**

32.0   *Impairment of extralinguistic functions*
         Includes : imitation (reproduction of sounds without com-
                 prehension)

32.1   *Impairment of processing, patterning, and retention of audi-
         tory stimuli in a temporal and form-integrated manner*

32.8   *Other impairment of sublinguistic functions*

32.9   *Unspecified*

33   **Impairment of other linguistic functions**

33.0   *Impairment of use of other language systems*
         Includes : finger spelling and sign language

33.1   *Impairment of listener feedback*
         Includes : lack of signals usually emitted by listener (e.g.,
                 affirmative nodding and phrases such as " I see
                 ...." and "Is that so ?")

33.2   *Other impairment of facial expression*
         Includes : increase, reduction, or inappropriateness of quantity
                 or range of facial expression (such as gaze avoidance,
                 looking up, and abnormal staring)
         Excludes : disturbance of facial expression (70.23)

33.3   *Other impairment of body language*
         Includes : pantomime, gesture, idiosyncratic or involuntary
                 patterns of body movement, and disturbance of
                 posture, orientation, and tonus (such as abnormally
                 reclined, relaxed, uncomfortable, inappropriate, or
                 closed posture position), uncommunicative body
                 orientation (e.g., turned away from conversation
                 partner at 90° angle), abnormally limited gesture,
                 abnormal muscle tension, agitation (e.g., fidgety,
                 restless, pacing, or frequent unnecessary move-
                 ments), and catatonic movements (echopraxia,
                 flexibilitas cerea, "Mitgehen", and echolalia)
         Excludes : slowness of body movement (28.0), sterotypies and
                 postural mannerisms (70.55), negativism (27.3), and
                 ambitendence (27.4)

33.4   *Other impairment of language comprehension, verbal*

33.5   *Other impairment of language comprehension*
         Includes : nonverbal

33.6   *Other impairment of language formulation, oral*

33.7   *Other impairment of language formulation*
Includes : graphic

33.8   *Other*

33.9   *Unspecified*

34   Other impairment of learning
Excludes : those related to impairment of intelligence (10-14),
and impairment of openness to new ideas (19.3)

34.0   *Delayed language comprehension and use for auditory stimuli*

34.1   *Delayed language comprehension and use for visual stimuli*

34.2   *Reading difficulties*

34.3   *Other impairment of reading*

34.4   *Impairment of writing*
Includes : mirror writing

34.5   *Other specific learning difficulties*
A child with specific learning difficulties is one with average or
above-average intelligence and with no evidence of major motor
disorder, neurosensory loss, primary emotional disorder, or environmental disadvantage, who exhibits difficulties in understanding or using spoken or written language as manifested by disorders
of listening, thinking, reading, writing, spelling, or arithmetic

34.8   *Other*

34.9   *Unspecified*

IMPAIRMENTS OF SPEECH (35-39)

35   Impairment of voice production

35.0   *Use of substitute voice*
Includes : artificial larynx

35.1   *Other deficiency of larynx*

35.2   *Other total loss of voice production*

35.3   *Severe dysarthria*

35.4   *Other dysarthria*

35.5 *Indistinct speech*
Includes : drawling, mumbling, slurring, and other features
making speech difficult to understand
Excludes : impairments of speech form (37)

35.6 *Other impairment of neurological control*
Includes : laryngeal palsy

35.7 *Other impairment of speech organs*

35.8 *Other*

35.9 *Unspecified*

36 Other impairment of voice function

36.0 *Other impairment of nonverbal "grammar"*
Includes : lack of changes of pitch and loudness to amplify
meaning
Excludes : impaired use of gesture (33.3)

36.1 *Impairment of voice modulation*
Includes : expressionless and flat tone of voice

36.2 *Impairment of pitch*

36.3 *Abnormally quiet voice*

36.4 *Other impairment of loudness*

36.5 *Other impairment of intonation*

36.6 *Impairment of voice quality*
Includes : harsh, breathy

36.7 *Impairment of other qualities of voice*

36.8 *Other*

36.9 *Unspecified*

37 Impairment of speech form

37.0 *Impairment of speech fluency*
Includes : stammering and stuttering

37.1 *Impairment of speech pressure*
Includes : more copious speech than normal, too rapid speech

37.2 *Other impairment of speech patterning*
Includes : impairment of rate, rhythm, and stress

37.3 *Other impairment of phonation*

37.4 *Other impairment of resonation*

37.5   *Impairment of coherence*
Includes : distorted grammar, lack of logical connexion, sudden irrelevancies, and answering off the point

37.6   *Nonsocial speech*
Includes : talking, muttering, or whispering out loud or out of context of conversation

37.7   *Other impairment of conversational form*
Includes : simultaneous talking or talking out of turn

37.8   *Other*

37.9   *Unspecified*

38   **Impairment of speech content**
Excludes : perseveration (17.4) and flight of ideas (17.7)

38.0   *Idiosyncratic use of words or phrases*
Includes : use of neologisms

38.1   *Other inappropriate speech*
Includes : excessive use of puns, rhymes, jokes, and song, and irrelevant speech

38.2   *Other impairment of humour*
Includes : other inappropriate humour or lack of humour although appropriate occasions offered by conversation

38.3   *Impairment of speech length*
Includes : abnormally lengthy or circumstantial speech, and individual difficult to interrupt

38.4   *Other impairment of speech quantity*
Includes : restricted quantity of speech (frequently fails to answer, or restricted to minimum necessary, or no extra sentences or additional comments)

38.5   *Poverty of speech content*

38.8   *Other*

38.9   *Unspecified*

39   **Other impairment of speech**

4   AURAL IMPAIRMENTS

Aural impairments relate not only to the ear, but also to its associated structures and functions. The most important subclass of aural impairment is made up of impairments relating to the function of hearing

IMPAIRMENTS OF AUDITORY SENSITIVITY (40-45)

Terminology The term "deaf" should be applied only to individuals whose hearing impairment is so severe that they are unable to benefit from any amplification
Auditory sensitivity is determined by the average hearing threshold level, measured in decibels (dB), for pure tone stimuli of 500, 1000, and 2000 hertz (Hz), with reference to ISO : R389 - 1970. Distinction is customarily made between the following levels of hearing impairment :

total hearing loss	
profound hearing impairment	more than 91 dB (ISO)
severe hearing impairment	71 - 91 dB (ISO)
moderately severe hearing impairment	56 - 70 dB (ISO)
moderate hearing impairment	41 - 55 dB (ISO)
mild hearing impairment	26 - 40 dB (ISO)

Coding Where hearing impairment is asymmetrical it should be classified according to the less impaired side.

40   Total or profound impairment of development of hearing

An individual who has lost or never had the ability to hear and understand speech even when amplified, this loss having been suffered prior to the age of 19 years
Includes : deaf mutism

41   Profound bilateral hearing loss

41.0   *Total bilateral hearing loss*

41.1   *Total hearing loss in one ear, profound impairment in the other ear*

41.2   *Profound bilateral impairment of hearing*

41.3   *Other profound hearing impairment of one ear specified as the better ear*

41.9   *Unspecified*
Includes :   (bilateral) deafness NOS, profound hearing loss NOS
Excludes :   profound hearing impairment where only one ear is mentioned and not specified as the better ear (44.3 and 44.7)

42   Profound hearing impairment in one ear with moderately severe impairment of the other ear

42.0   *Total hearing loss in one ear, hearing impairment of other ear severe*

42.1   *Total hearing loss in one ear, hearing impairment of other ear moderately severe*

42.2   *Profound hearing impairment in one ear, hearing impairment of other ear severe*

42.3   *Profound hearing impairment in one ear, hearing impairment of other ear moderately severe*

42.4   *Other severe hearing impairment in one ear specified as the better ear*

43   Moderately severe bilateral hearing impairment

43.0   *Severe bilateral hearing impairment*

43.1   *Severe hearing impairment in one ear, hearing impairment in other ear moderately severe*

43.2   *Moderately severe bilateral hearing impairment*

43.3   *Other moderately severe hearing impairment in one ear specified as the better ear*

43.8   *Hard of hearing bilaterally NOS*

43.9   *Unspecified*
Includes :   bilateral hearing impairment NOS, hard of hearing NOS, psychogenic deafness
Excludes :   moderately severe hearing impairment where only one ear mentioned and not specified as the better ear (45.1, 45.3)

44   **Profound hearing impairment in one ear with moderate or lesser impairment of the other ear**

44.0   *Total hearing loss in one ear, hearing impairment in other ear moderate*

44.1   *Total hearing loss in one ear, hearing impairment in other ear mild*

44.2   *Total hearing loss in one ear, no hearing impairment in other ear*

44.3   *Total hearing loss in one ear, hearing impairment in other ear not stated*

44.4   *Profound hearing impairment in one ear, hearing impairment in other ear moderate*

44.5   *Profound hearing impairment in one ear, hearing impairment in other ear mild*

44.6   *Profound hearing impairment in one ear, no hearing impairment in other ear*

44.7   *Profound hearing impairment in one ear, hearing impairment in other ear not stated*

44.9   *Unspecified*
Includes : deafness of one ear NOS

45   **Other impairment of auditory sensitivity**

45.0   *Severe hearing impairment in one ear, hearing impairment in other ear moderate or mild*

45.1   *Severe hearing impairment in one ear, hearing impairment in other ear not present or not stated*

45.2   *Moderately severe hearing impairment in one ear, hearing impairment in other ear moderate or mild*

45.3   *Moderately severe hearing impairment in one ear, hearing impairment in other ear not present or not stated*

45.4   *Moderate bilateral hearing impairment*

45.5   *Moderate hearing impairment in one ear, hearing impairment in other ear mild*

45.6   *Moderate hearing impairment in one ear, hearing impairment in other ear not present or not stated*

45.7   *Mild bilateral hearing impairment*

45.8   *Mild hearing impairment in one ear, hearing impairment in other ear not present or not stated*

45.9   *Unspecified*
        Includes : hearing impairment NOS

OTHER AUDITORY AND AURAL IMPAIRMENTS (46-49)

46   Impairment of speech discrimination
        A distortion of hearing function where the basic problem exists
        in discrimination and recognition, involving auditory distortion
        not accountable in terms of sensorineural sensitivity. It is assessed
        by speech audiometry (discrimination for monosyllabic words in
        quiet, with speech presented at comfort level in sound field), but
        is a function of auditory sensitivity and can be calculated from
        the pure tone threshold of hearing, and so often is not distinguished
        Excludes : impairments accompanied by impairment of
                     auditory sensitivity (40-45)

46.0   *Profound bilateral impairment of discrimination* (less than 40%
        correct)

46.1   *Severe bilateral impairment of discrimination* (40-49% correct)

46.2   *Moderately severe bilateral impairment of discrimination* (50-59%
        correct)

46.3   *Moderate bilateral impairment of discrimination* (60-79% correct)

46.4   *Mild bilateral impairment of discrimination* (80-90 % correct)

46.5   *Profound unilateral impairment of discrimination* (less than 40%
        correct)

46.6   *Severe or moderately severe unilateral impairment of discrimi-
        nation* (40-59% correct)

46.7   *Moderate or mild unilateral impairment of discrimination*
        (60-90% correct)

46.8   *Other and unspecified bilateral impairment of discrimination*
        Includes : where correctness not quantified but specified as
                     bilateral

46.9   *Other and unspecified*
        Includes : where correctness not quantified

47   Other impairment of auditory function

47.0   *Impairment of sound conduction NEC*

47.1   *Sensorineural impairment NEC*

47.2   *Tinnitus*

47.3   *Other subjective impairments of hearing*
47.4 * *Mixed impairment of auditory function*
47.8   *Other impairment of auditory function*
47.9   *Unspecified*

48   Impairment of vestibular and balance function

48.0   *Vertigo*
        Includes : dizziness
48.1   *Impairment of labyrinthine function*
48.2   *Impairment of locomotion related to vestibular or cerebellar function*
48.3   *Other impairment of cerebellar and coordinating function*
48.4   *Other impairment of vestibular function*
48.5   *Liability to falls*
        Includes : those occurring suddenly while walking, giving rise
                    to a tendency to walk holding on to furniture and
                    associated with rejection of human help
        Excludes : impulsive falls (48.6)
48.6   *Impulsive falls*
        Includes : the impulsive elderly individual who gets up and tries
                    to walk and then overbalances and falls (i.e., is able
                    to walk but requires supervision because of the risk
                    of falling)
48.7   *Other impairment of balance*
48.8   *Other*
        Excludes : impairment of coordination of limbs (74)
48.9   *Unspecified*

49   Other impairment of aural function

49.0   *Deficiency of inner ear*
49.1   *Deformity of inner ear*
49.2   *Aural discharge*
        Includes : otorrhoea
49.3   *Aural irritation*
        Includes : dermatitis and ear pain
49.4   *Other aural infection*
49.5   *Deficiency of middle ear*
49.6   *Deformity of middle ear*

49.7   *Deformity of external ear*
        Includes : deficiency and disfigurement
49.8   *Other impairment of external ear*
49.9   *Other and unspecified*

5   OCULAR IMPAIRMENTS

Ocular impairments relate not only to the eye, but also to its associated structures and functions, including the eyelids. The most important subclass of ocular impairment is made up of impairments relating to the function of vision

IMPAIRMENTS OF VISUAL ACUITY (50-55)

Scope   The degree of impairment may be reduced by compensating aids, and a refractive error that can be fully corrected by glasses or contact lenses is generally not regarded as a visual impairment. However, provision for identifying such individuals has been made in category 57.0

Terminology   Different meanings are attached to the term "blindness", particularly in the context of legal definitions. In order to avoid ambiguity a preferred nomenclature for visual impairments is defined in the table, in which synonymous terms are also identified

Coding
1.   The degree of impairment may be different for the two eyes of an individual. Unfortunately there is no consistency in identifying these differences — sometimes the performance of both eyes is recorded, sometimes only that of what is specified as the better or the worse eye, and sometimes only that of one eye without further qualification. A reference chart is appended after category 55

2.   Absence of an eye is classified separately from other profound impairments of visual function. This distinction is made because the individual with a missing eye is additionally impaired in regard to appearance, i.e., he has a disfiguring deficiency

3   As the reference chart indicates, provision is made for all possible combinations of impairments of visual acuity; multiple coding within this section is therefore unnecessary

TERMINOLOGY FOR IMPAIRMENTS OF VISUAL ACUITY

WHO category of vision	Degree of impairment	Visual acuity (with best possible correction)	Synonyms and alternative definitions
NORMAL VISION	None	0.8 or better ($5/6, 6/7.5, 20/25$, or better)	range of normal vision
	Slight	less than 0.8 (< $5/6, 6/7.5$, or $20/25$)	near-normal vision
LOW VISION	Moderate	less than 0.3 (< $5/15, 6/18$ or $6/20$, or $20/80$ or $20/70$)	moderate low vision
	Severe	less than 0.12 (< $5/40, 6/48$, or $20/160$) (< $0.1, 5/50, 6/60$, or $20/200$)§	severe low vision – legal blindness in some countries; count fingers at 6 m or less
BLINDNESS ¶	Profound	less than 0.05 (< $5/100, 3/60$, or $20/400$)	profound low vision or moderate blindness – blindness in ICD-9; count fingers at less than 3 m – finger counting NOS
	Near-total	less than 0.02 (≤ $5/300, 1/60$, or $3/200$)	severe or near-total blindness; count fingers at 1 m or less, or hand motions at 5 m or less, or hand motions NOS, or light perception
	Total	no light perception (NLP)	total blindness (including absence of eye)

§   this alternative level of visual acuity is less accurate : on charts without lines at 0.16 and 0.12 it means effectively < 0.2.

¶   one or both eyes.

50   Absence of eye

50.0   *Absence of both eyes*

50.1   *Absence of one eye, visual impairment of other eye total*

50.2   *Absence of one eye, visual impairment of other eye near-total*

50.3   *Absence of one eye, visual impairment of other eye profound*

50.4   *Absence of one eye, visual impairment of other eye severe*

50.5   *Absence of one eye, visual impairment of other eye moderate*

50.6   *Absence of one eye, visual impairment of other eye slight*

50.7   *Absence of one eye, no visual impairment of other eye*

50.8   *Other absence of one eye*
        Includes :   absence of one eye when degree of visual performance
                        in other eye not specified

50.9   *Unspecified*

51   Profound visual impairment of both eyes
        (see chart after category 55)

51.0   *Total visual impairment of both eyes*

51.1   *Total visual impairment of one eye, visual impairment of other eye
        near-total*

51.2   *Total visual impairment of one eye, visual impairment of other eye
        profound*

51.3   *Near-total visual impairment of both eyes*

51.4   *Near-total visual impairment of one eye, visual impairment of other
        eye profound*

51.5   *Other near-total visual impairment of one eye specified as the better
        eye*

51.6   *Profound visual impairment of both eyes*

51.7   *Other profound visual impairment of one eye specified as the better
        eye*

51.9   *Unspecified*
        Includes : (bilateral) blindness NOS
        Excludes :   profound visual impairment where only one eye mentioned
                        and not specified as the better eye (54.2, 54.5, and 54.8)

52   Profound visual impairment of one eye with low vision in the other eye
        (see chart after category 55)

52.0   *Total visual impairment of one eye, visual impairment of other eye
        severe*

52.1   *Total visual impairment of one eye, visual impairment of other eye
        moderate*

52.2   *Near-total visual impairment of one eye, visual impairment of other
        eye severe*

52.3   *Near-total visual impairment of one eye, visual impairment of other
        eye moderate*

52.4   *Profound visual impairment of one eye, visual impairment of other
        eye severe*

52.5   *Profound visual impairment of one eye, visual impairment of other
        eye moderate*

52.6   *Other severe visual impairment of one eye specified as the better eye*

52.9   *Unspecified*
        Includes : blindness (WHO category) of one eye and low vision of
                other eye NOS

53   Moderate visual impairment of both eyes
        (see chart after category 55)

53.0   *Severe visual impairment of both eyes*
53.1   *Severe visual impairment of one eye, visual impairment of other
        eye moderate*
53.2   *Moderate visual impairment of both eyes*
53.3   *Other moderate visual impairment of one eye specified as the
        better eye*
53.8   *Low vision of both eyes NOS*
53.9   *Unspecified*
        Includes : bilateral visual impairment NOS, low vision NOS
        Excludes : moderate visual impairment where only one eye
                    mentioned and not specified as the better eye
                    (55.2, 55.5, and 55.8)

54   Profound visual impairment of one eye
        (see chart after category 55)

54.0   *Total visual impairment of one eye, visual impairment of other
        eye slight*
54.1   *Total visual impairment of one eye, no visual impairment of
        other eye*
54.2   *Total visual impairment of one eye, visual impairment of other
        eye not stated*
54.3   *Near-total visual impairment of one eye, visual impairment of
        other eye slight*
54.4   *Near-total visual impairment of one eye, no visual impairment of
        other eye*
54.5   *Near-total visual impairment of one eye, visual impairment of
        other eye not stated*
54.6   *Profound visual impairment of one eye, visual impairment of
        other eye slight*
54.7   *Profound visual impairment of one eye, no visual impairment
        of other eye*
54.8   *Profound visual impairment of one eye, visual impairment of
        other eye not stated*

54.9 *Unspecified*
Includes : blindness of one eye NOS

55 Other impairment of visual acuity
(see chart below)

55.0 *Severe visual impairment of one eye, visual impairment of other eye slight*

55.1 *Severe visual impairment of one eye, no visual impairment of other eye*

55.2 *Severe visual impairment of one eye, visual impairment of other eye not stated*

55.3 *Moderate visual impairment of one eye, visual impairment of other eye slight*

55.4 *Moderate visual impairment of one eye, no visual impairment of other eye*

55.5 *Moderate visual impairment of one eye, visual impairment of other eye not stated*

55.6 *Slight visual impairment of both eyes*

55.7 *Slight visual impairment of one eye, no visual impairment of other eye*

55.8 *Slight visual impairment of one eye, visual impairment of other eye not stated*

55.9 *Unspecified*
Includes : (unilateral) impairment of vision NOS, loss of vision NOS

REFERENCE CHART FOR CLASSIFICATION OF IMPAIRMENTS OF VISUAL ACUITY §

Degree of impair-ment of better eye	Degree of impairment of other eye						
	total	near-total	profound	severe	moderate	slight	not specified
total	51.0						
near-total	51.1	51.3					51.5
profound	51.2	51.4	51.6				51.7
severe	52.0	52.2	52.4	53.0			52.6
moderate	52.1	52.3	52.5	53.1	53.2		53.3
slight	54.0	54.3	54.6	55.0	55.3	55.6	
none	54.1	54.4	54.7	55.1	55.4	55.7	
better eye not specified	54.2	54.5	54.8	55.2	55.5	55.8	

§ excludes where an eye is absent (50), or where only WHO categories of vision specified (51.9, 53.8, 54.9)

OTHER VISUAL AND OCULAR IMPAIRMENTS (56-58)

Excludes : central disorders of visual function
(30.1, 31.0, and 31.2)

56   Visual field impairment
Excludes : impairments accompanied by impairment of visual acuity
(50-55)

56.0   *Total impairment of visual fields* (field diameter 0°)

56.1   *Near-total impairment of visual fields* (field diameter 5° or less)

56.2   *Profound impairment of visual fields* (field diameter 10° or less)

56.3   *Severe impairment of visual fields* (field diameter 20° or less)

56.4   *Moderate impairment of visual fields* (field diameter 60° or less)

56.5   *Slight impairment of visual fields* (field diameter 120° or less)

56.6   *Tunnel vision NOS*

56.7   *Hemianopia*

56.8   *Other unilateral visual field impairment*

56.9   *Other and unspecified*

57   Other visual impairment

57.0   *Wears correcting lenses* (with resultant normal or near-normal vision)

57.1   *Astigmatism*

57.2   *Impairment of visual accommodation*

57.3   *Diplopia*
Includes : strabismus

57.4   *Other impairment of ocular motility and binocular vision*
Includes : nystagmus

57.5   *Impairment of colour vision*

57.6   *Impairment of night vision*

57.7   *Subjective impairment of vision*
Includes : amblyopia, distortions, floaters, and transient visual
loss
Excludes : blurred vision, eye pain, and eye strain (58.7)

57.8   *Other impairment of vision*
Includes : light sensitivity

57.9   *Unspecified*

58   Other ocular impairment

58.0   *Ocular discharge*
Includes : excessive lacrimal secretion, running eye

58.1   *Other ocular infection*

58.2   *Anaesthetic eye*

58.3   *Dry eye*
        Includes : irritating eye

58.4   *Deformity of eyeball*
        Includes : disfigurement and exophthalmos
        Excludes : absence of eyeball (50)

58.5   *Deformity of eyelid*
        Includes :   blepharitis, everted eyelids, ptosis, and deficiency or
                     disfigurement of eyelids

58.6   *Other impairment of eyelid*

58.7   *Ill-defined ocular impairment*
        Includes : blurred vision, eye pain, eye strain

58.8   *Other ocular impairment*

58.9   *Unspecified*

6   VISCERAL IMPAIRMENTS

Visceral impairments include impairments of internal organs and of other special functions. The array of underlying disorders that may give rise to these impairments is very considerable, extending over large sections of the ICD. However, the functional consequences of such disorders are much more limited. For instance, cardiovascular and respiratory diseases occupy 129 categories in two chapters of the ICD, but their common functional consequences can be identified comprehensively within a single two-digit category of the impairment classification.

IMPAIRMENTS OF INTERNAL ORGANS (60-66)

60   Mechanical and motor impairment of internal organs

60.0   *Tracheobronchial obstruction*

60.1   *Oesophageal or gastric obstruction*

60.2   *Intestinal obstruction*

60.3   *Other mechanical impairment of internal organs*
        Excludes :   urinary obstruction (63.4) and genital obstruction
              (66.5)

60.4   *Diaphragmatic palsy*

60.5   *Other motor or analogous functional impairment of internal organs*
        Excludes :   laryngeal palsy (35.6)

60.8 *   *Combinations of the above*

60.9   *Unspecified*

61   Impairment of cardiorespiratory function
        Excludes :   syncope (21.6), peripheral manifestations classifiable to disfigurements of head (82) and of limbs (84-87) such as cyanosis and oedema, and gangrene (99.1-99.3)

61.0   *Shortness of breath*
        Includes :   dyspnoea, orthopnoea, and respiratory failure

61.1   *Other disturbance of breathing*
        Includes :   stridor and wheezing

61.2   *Other abnormal sounds*
        Includes :   cardiac murmurs and abnormal sounds in chest

61.3   *Exercise pain in chest*

61.4   *Other chest pain*

61.5   *Other exercise intolerance*
Includes : intermittent claudication
Excludes : fatigue (94.6) and pain on exercise in arm (97.3)

61.6   *Disturbance of cardiac rhythm*
Includes : arrhythmia, heart block, palpitation, and tachycardia

61.7   *Cough or sputum*

61.8   *Other impairment of cardiorespiratory function*
Includes : haemoptysis
Excludes : subject to corrective or prosthetic intervention or
          surgery (65.20)

61.9   *Unspecified*

62   Impairment of gastrointestinal function
Excludes : impairment of mastication and swallowing (68) ꞌ

62.0   *Food intolerance*
Includes : nausea
Excludes : specific dietary intolerance (93.2) and anorexia (25.0)

62.1   *Vomiting and regurgitation*

62.2   *Flatulence*
Includes : borborygmi, eructation, and hiccough

62.3   *Abdominal pain*
Includes : intestinal colic and biliary colic

62.4   *Constipation*

62.5   *Diarrhoea*

62.6   *Irritable colon*

62.7   *Other intestinal functional impairment*
Includes : gastrointestinal hypermotility, dumping, and intestinal
          hurry

62.8   *Other impairment of gastrointestinal function*
Includes : piles and rectal bleeding, mucus, and pain
Excludes : severe impairment of continence (91)

62.9   *Unspecified*
Includes : faecal incontinence NOS

63   Impairment of urinary function

63.0   *Renal colic*

63.1   *Other impairment of renal function*
Includes : renal failure
Excludes : renal dialysis (94.0) and transplantation (65.60)

63.2   *Frequency of micturition*
Includes : polyuria

63.3   *Reflex incontinence*
Voluntary loss of urine due to abnormal reflex activity in the
spinal cord in the absence of the sensation usually associated
with the desire to micturate
Includes : automatic bladder

63.4   *Overflow incontinence*
Involuntary loss of urine when the intravesical pressure exceeds
the maximum urethral pressure owing to an elevation of intravesical pressure associated with bladder distension but in the
absence of detrusor activity
Includes : outflow obstruction of micturition, and prostatism

63.5   *Urge incontinence*
Involuntary loss of urine associated with a strong desire to void ;
it may be motor, associated with uninhibited detrusor contractions, or sensory, not due to uninhibited detrusor contractions

63.6   *Stress incontinence*
Involuntary loss of urine when the intravesical pressure exceeds
the maximum urethral pressure but in the absence of detrusor
activity

63.7   *Other impairment of micturition*
Includes : dysuria

63.8   *Other impairment of urinary function*
Excludes : severe impairment of continence (91)

63.9   *Unspecified*

64   **Impairment of reproductive function**
Excludes : impairment of sexual organs (67), impotence
(25.40), and frigidity (25.42)

64.0   *Currently subject to contraceptive procedure*
Includes : consuming a contraceptive pill, intrauterine device *in
situ*, and post-vasectomy

64.1   *Sterility*
Excludes : impairments of internal genitalia (65.8 and 66.5)

64.2   *Subfertility*
Includes : infertility other than that due to sterility

64.3   *Dyspareunia*
        Excludes : that related to vaginal discharge (67.3)

64.4   *Sexual ambiguity*
        Includes : hermaphroditism

64.5   *Dysmenorrhoea*

64.6   *Menorrhagia*
        Includes : vaginal bleeding and excessive menstrual loss

64.8   *Other disturbance of menstrual function*

64.9   *Other and unspecified*

65   Deficiency of internal organs

65.0   *Deficiency of tracheobronchial tree*
        Excludes : deficiency of larynx (35.1)

65.1   *Deficiency of lung*

65.2   *Deficiency of heart*

        65.20   subject to corrective or prosthetic intervention
                  or surgery
                  Excludes : pacemaker (94.0)

        65.21   anomalies of cardiac development (such as patent
                  interventricular septum)

        65.22   acquired valvular lesions

        65.28   other

        65.29   unspecified

65.3   *Deficiency of oesophagus and stomach*

65.4   *Deficiency of intestine and rectum*

65.5   *Deficiency of gall bladder, liver, or spleen*

65.6   *Deficiency of kidney*

        65.60   subject to renal transplantation

        65.68   other

        65.69   unspecified

65.7   *Deficiency of bladder*

65.8   *Deficiency of internal genitalia*

65.9   *Other and unspecified*

66   Other impairment of internal organs
        Excludes : artificial and abnormal orifices (88)

66.0 *Abnormality of blood vessels of thorax and abdomen*
Includes : aortic aneurysm

66.1 *Haemorrhage from internal organs*
Includes : pulmonary, intrathoracic, gastrointestinal, and intra-
abdominal
Excludes : epistaxis (69.3), haemoptysis (61.8), and rectal bleeding (62.8)

66.2 *Transposition of viscera*
Includes : situs inversus viscerum

66.3 *Accessory viscera*
Includes : splenunculus

66.4 *Other structural abnormality of viscera*
Excludes : deficiencies (65)

66.5 *Other impairment of internal genitalia*
Includes : tubal obstruction
Excludes : deficiency (65.8) and malpositioning (67.4, 67.5)

66.8 *Other impairments of internal organs*

66.9 *Unspecified*

IMPAIRMENTS OF OTHER SPECIAL FUNCTIONS (67-69)

67   Impairment of sexual organs

67.0 *Absence of nipples*

67.1 *Hypertrophy of breasts*

67.2 *Other impairment of nipples and breasts*

67.3 *Genital discharge*
Includes : urethritis, vaginitis, and urethral or vaginal discharge
or irritation

67.4 *Prolapse*
Includes : procidentia

67.5 *Other malposition of internal sex organs*
Includes : undescended testicle

67.6 *Other deformity or deficiency of external genitalia*
Includes : hypospadias

67.7 *Other impairment of external genitalia*

67.8 *Other impairment of sexual organs*

67.9 *Unspecified*

68   Impairment of mastication and swallowing
Excludes : impairment of jaw (70) and dentofacial impairments (80)

68.0   *Currently wearing dental prosthesis*

68.1   *Deficiency of teeth, complete*
Includes : edentulous
Excludes : if wearing prosthesis (68.0)

68.2   *Other deficiency of teeth*
Includes : caries or decay
Excludes : if wearing prosthesis (68.0)

68.3   *Toothache*

68.4   *Impairment of salivation*
Includes : dry mouth

68.5   *Other impairment of salivary function*

68.6   *Other impairment of mastication*

68.7   *Other impairment of swallowing*

68.8   *Other*

68.9   *Unspecified*

69   Impairment related to olfaction and other special functions

69.0   *Impairment of smell and taste*

69.1   *Impairment of smell*

69.2   *Impairment of taste*

69.3   *Nasal discharge*
Includes : epistaxis and rhinorrhoea

69.4   *Nasal obstruction*

69.5   *Other impairment of nasal function*
Excludes : nasal deficiency (80.6) and nasal deformity (81.0)

69.8   *Impairment of other special functions*
Excludes : impairment of sleep (22)

69.9   *Unspecified*

7   SKELETAL IMPAIRMENTS

Skeletal impairments have been interpreted broadly so as to reflect the disposition of the body and its visible parts. Skeletal impairments include mechanical and motor disturbances of the face, head, neck, trunk, and limbs, as well as deficiencies of the limbs. Recourse to a fourth-digit has often been necessary in order to encompass the level of detail desired

> Excludes :   certain more evidently disfiguring impairments (80-87)

IMPAIRMENTS OF HEAD AND TRUNK REGIONS (70)

70   **Impairment of head and trunk regions**
Excludes :   most deficiencies and disfigurements (80-83)

70.1   *Mechanical and motor impairment of jaw*

	70.10	Trismus
	70.11	Malocclusion
	70.12	Prognathism
	70.13	Underdevelopment of lower jaw
	70.14	Other disturbance of jaw development
	70.15	Other jaw dysfunctions
		Includes : clicking
	70.18	Other
	70.19	Unspecified

70.2   *Mechanical and motor impairment of face*

	70.20	Facial paralysis
		Includes : facial palsy
	70.21	Involuntary facial movements
		Includes : tics and masticatory movements
	70.22	Other facial mannerisms
		Includes : stereotypies and distinct idiosyncratic or repetitive movements of unclear meaning not classifiable as tics or automatisms (e.g., constant repetition of movements, or postures such as rubbing and grimacing)
	70.23	Other disturbance of facial expression
		Excludes : impairment of facial expression (33.2)
	70.28	Other
	70.29	Unspecified

70.3   *Other mechanical and motor impairment of head*

    70.30   Mechanical impairment of head

    70.31   Abnormal movement of head
             Includes : titubation

    70.32   Other motor impairment of head

    70.38   Other
             Includes : both mechanical and motor impairments
                        of head

    70.39   Unspecified

70.4   *Mechanical and motor impairment of neck*

    70.40   Torticollis

    70.41   Other mechanical impairment of neck

    70.42   Other motor impairment of neck

    70.48   Other
             Includes : both mechanical and motor impairments
                        of neck

    70.49   Unspecified

70.5   *Impairment of posture*

    70.50   Spinal curvature
             Includes : kyphosis, lordosis, and scoliosis

    70.51   Deficiency of vertebra

    70.52   Other deficiency of spine

    70.53   Other spinal deformity

    70.54   Involuntary body movements
             Includes : dyskinesia and dystonia
             Excludes : those of limbs (74)

    70.55   Postural mannerisms
             Includes : odd stylized movements or acts (usually
                        idiosyncratic and often suggestive of
                        special meaning or purpose) and stereo-
                        typies (constant repetition of movements
                        or postures such as rocking, rubbing, and
                        nodding)
             Excludes : other impairments of body language (33.3)

    70.58   Other

    70.59   Unspecified

70.6   *Impairment of physique*

    70.60   Dwarfism
             Includes : short stature
             Excludes : generalized skeletal defect (70.65)

70.61 Gigantism
Includes : unduly tall stature

70.62 Other impairment of stature

70.63 Emaciation
Includes : undue thinness

70.64 Obesity

70.65 Generalized skeletal defect
Includes : achondroplasia

70.68 Other

70.69 Unspecified

70.7 *Other mechanical and motor impairment of trunk*

70.70 Impairment of pelvis potentially interfering with normal delivery
Includes : contracted pelvis
Excludes : deficiency of pelvis (75.4 and 78.0-78.2)

70.71 Other impairment of skeletal structures of trunk NEC

70.72 Other abnormality of tissues in trunk region NEC

70.78 Other

70.79 Unspecified

70.8 *Other impairment of head and trunk region NEC*
Includes : reduced plasticity or slowing of physical functions encountered in association with ageing

70.9 *Unspecified*

MECHANICAL AND MOTOR IMPAIRMENTS OF LIMBS (71-74)

As elsewhere in this section, differentiation is made between mechanical and motor impairments. The distinction is analogous to that between the physical state of a piece of machinery and its constituent parts on the one hand, and that of the power source and its transmission on the other.

Throughout this section certain terms are used with particular meanings :

extent of involvement : *complete* if there is involvement of the whole of a limb, and

incomplete if only part of a limb is affected

degree of involvement : *total* if the attribute is totally lacking, and
partial if there is a reduction of the attribute

71   Mechanical impairment of limb

The following fourth-digit subclassification to indicate the nature of the mechanical impairment is suggested for use with categories 71.0-71.7

0   total loss of movement, with or without deformity, bilateral
Includes : ankylosis and fixation specified as bilateral

1   other total loss of movement
Includes : ankylosis and fixation

2   instability, bilateral
Includes : flail joint specified as bilateral

3   other instability
Includes : flail joint

4   other deformity, including deviation of axis, bilateral
Excludes : with fixation (0, above)

5   other deformity
Excludes : with fixation (1, above)., or if congenital (84)

6   other restriction or loss of movement, bilateral
Includes : stiffness related to mechanical impairment bilaterally
Excludes : congenital contracture (84)

7   other restriction or loss of movement
Includes : dislocation, and stiffness related to mechanical impairment

8 *   mixed impairment
(e.g., otherwise classifiable to 1, above, on one side and 7, above, on other)

9   unspecified

71.0   *Mechanical impairment of shoulder and upper arm*

71.1   *Mechanical impairment of elbow and forearm*

71.2   *Mechanical impairment of wrist and carpus*
Excludes : impairment also involving the hand (71.3)

71.3   *Mechanical impairment of metacarpus and hand*
Includes : impairment also involving the wrist and carpus

71.4   *Mechanical impairment of finger*
Includes : impairment of thumb
Excludes : impairment of finger if hand also impaired (71.3)

71.5   *Mechanical impairment of hip and thigh*

71.6   *Mechanical impairment of knee and leg*

71.7   *Mechanical impairment of ankle and foot*
        Includes : impairment of subtaloid, tarsal, and metatarsal joints
        Excludes : toes (71.90 and 71.91)

71.8   *Mixed and other upper limb mechanical impairment*
        Excludes : impairments classifiable to 71.08 *, 71.18 *, 71.28 *,
                   71.38 *, and 71.48 *

    71.80 *   Mechanical impairment of more than one region of
                   an upper limb or limbs
                   Includes : shoulder-hand syndrome

    71.81 *   Upper arm impairment on one side with forearm impair-
                   ment on the other

    71.82 *   Upper arm impairment on one side with wrist or hand
                   impairment on the other

    71.83 *   Upper arm impairment on one side with finger impair-
                   ment on the other

    71.84 *   Forearm impairment on one side with wrist or hand
                   impairment on the other

    71.85 *   Forearm impairment on one side with finger impair-
                   ment on the other

    71.86 *   Wrist or hand impairment on one side with finger im-
                   pairment on the other

    71.88 *   Other mixed mechanical impairment of upper limb

    71.89   Other and unspecified mechanical impairment of upper
                   limb

71.9   *Mixed and other mechanical impairment of limb*
        Excludes : impairments classifiable to 71.58 *, 71.68 *, 71.78 *,
                   and 71.8

    71.90   Mechanical impairment of toes, bilateral

    71.91   Other mechanical impairment of toes

    71.92   Impairment of lower limbs due to unequal length of
                   legs NEC

    71.93   Other and unspecified mechanical impairment of lower
                   limb
                   Includes : impairment of walking NOS

    71.94 *   Hip or thigh impairment on one side with knee or leg
                   impairment on the other

    71.95 *   Hip or thigh impairment on one side with ankle, foot,
                   or toe impairment on the other

71.96 *   Knee or leg impairment on one side with ankle, foot, or toe impairment on the other

71.97 *   Other mixed mechanical impairment of lower limb

71.98 *   Mixed mechanical impairment of upper and lower limb

71.99   Unspecified mechanical impairment of limb

72   Spastic paralysis of more than one limb
Includes : hemiplegia, paraplegia, and tetraplegia

72.0   *Complete spastic paralysis of upper and lower limbs on same side, with involvement of speech*
Includes : (spastic) hemiplegia, dominant side or with involvement of speech

72.1   *Other complete spastic paralysis of upper and lower limbs on same side*

72.2   *Other spastic paralysis of upper and lower limb on same side*
Includes : (spastic) hemiparesis

72.3   *Bilateral complete paralysis of lower limbs*
Includes : (spastic) paraplegia

72.4   *Other bilateral spastic paralysis of lower limbs*
Includes : (spastic) paraparesis

72.5   *Spastic paralysis of three limbs*

72.6   *Complete paralysis of all four limbs*
Includes : (spastic) tetraplegia

72.7   *Other spastic paralysis of all four limbs*
Includes : (spastic) tetraparesis

72.8   *Other spastic paralysis of more than one limb*

72.9   *Unspecified*

73   Other paralysis of limb

The following fourth-digit subclassification to indicate the nature of the paralysis is suggested for use with categories 73.0-73.9

0   complete spastic paralysis
Excludes : paralysis classifiable to 72.0, 72.1, 72.3, and 72.6

1   other spastic paralysis
Excludes : paralysis classifiable to 72.2, 72.4, 72.5, and 72.8

2	complete total flaccid paralysis
3	other total flaccid paralysis
4	complete partial flaccid paralysis
5	other flaccid paralysis
6	other weakness of limb
7	fatigue of limb
9	unspecified

73.0 *Bilateral paralysis of upper limbs*

73.1 *Paralysis of dominant upper limb*

73.2 *Other paralysis of upper limb*

73.3 *Bilateral paralysis of lower limbs*
Excludes : paralysis classifiable to 72.3 and 72.4

73.4 *Other paralysis of lower limb*

73.5 *Paralysis of upper and lower limbs on same side*
Excludes : paralysis classifiable to 72.0, 72.1, and 72.2

73.6 *Paralysis of three limbs*
Excludes : paralysis classifiable to 72.5

73.7 *Paralysis of all four limbs*
Excludes : paralysis classifiable to 72.6 and 72.7

73.8 *Other paralysis*

73.80	Spastic paralysis, complete
73.81	Other spastic paralysis
	Includes : spastic paresis or paralysis NOS
73.82	Total flaccid paralysis, complete
73.83	Other total flaccid paralysis
73.84	Partial flaccid paralysis, complete
73.85	Other flaccid paralysis
	Includes : flaccid paralysis NOS
73.86	Other weakness of limbs
73.87	Fatigue of limbs
	Excludes : fatigue NOS (94.5)

73.9 *Unspecified*

74   Other motor impairment of limb
Excludes : stiffness related to mechanical impairment (71)

The following fourth-digit subclassification to indicate the nature of the impairment is suggested for use with this category :

	0	rigidity or stiffness, complete
	1	other rigidity or stiffness
	2	abnormal movement, complete
		Includes : tremor
	3	other abnormal movement
	4	lack of coordination, complete
	5	other lack of coordination
	6	other impairment of dexterity
	7	other
	8 *	mixed
		(e.g., otherwise classifiable as both 0 and 5, above)
	9	unspecified

74.0   *Other bilateral motor impairment of upper limbs*

74.1   *Other motor impairment of dominant upper limb*

74.2   *Other motor impairment of upper limb*

74.3   *Other bilateral motor impairment of lower limbs*

74.4   *Other motor impairment of lower limb*

74.5   *Other motor impairment of upper and lower limbs on same side*

    74.50   Hemiballismus

74.6   *Other motor impairment involving three or four limbs*

74.8   *Other motor impairment*

74.9   *Unspecified*

    74.92   Tremor NOS

    74.97   Limping NOS
             Excludes : impairment of walking NOS (71.93)

DEFICIENCIES OF LIMBS (75-79)

Excludes : other congenital malformations of limbs (84 and 85)

Scope   *Transverse deficiencies* (75-76) present essentially as an
         amputation-like stump; they may arise as a failure of
         formation of parts, or as the result of surgical inter-
         vention. These impairments include those previously
         designated as peromelia or terminal transverse deficien-
         cies. A deficiency is customarily identified by the level
         at which the limb terminates (the most proximal part
         that is missing), it being understood that all elements
         distal to the level named are also absent

Excludes : where a deficiency is not complete across the
limb at the same level (when it is probably
longitudinal rather than transverse)

Longitudinal deficiencies (77-79). All skeletal limb deficiencies other than those of the transverse type should be
placed in the longitudinal category, though by the same
token almost all arise as a failure of formation of parts.
These impairments include those previously designated as
ectromelias or terminal longitudinal, intercalary transverse,
and intercalary longitudinal deficiencies. All absent bones
or portions of bones that are missing are named, any bones
not named as being missing being understood to be present

Terminology The International Society for Prosthetics and Orthotics
(ISPO) has developed a preferred nomenclature and recommended abbreviations for describing the appropriate
levels, and these have been incorporated in the classification

Coding 1 A reference chart is appended after category 79, indicating the equivalence between preferred and previous
nomenclatures

2 The terms "complete" and "incomplete" have been
used with consistency throughout the classification
to indicate the extent of an impairment, "complete"
denoting involvement of the whole of the part and
"incomplete" that less than the whole of the part is
affected. However, in practice the terms "total" and
"partial" may be encountered and in this context
they should be interpreted as equivalent to
"complete" and "incomplete" respectively

3 ISPO has a strong preference for full specification of deficiencies, which calls for multiple coding. As a result only
a very limited provision for combination categories has
been incorporated for other users

4 The degree of detail that is desirable varies in relation to
the structure of the part affected. Thus,in proximal parts,
particularly those related to long bones, it is the level of
the deficiency that is of most concern. In contrast, in
distal parts with greater transverse differentiation it is
the ray manifesting the deficiency that is of greater interest. For this reason separate subclassifications have
been developed for deficiencies of proximal parts, 75, 77,
78, and for those of distal parts, 76 and 79

75   **Transverse deficiency of proximal parts of limb**
(see chart after category 79)
Includes : those of arm, carpus, leg, and tarsus

The following fourth-digit subclassification to indicate the extent
of the deficiency is recommended for use with this category :

0   complete deficiency, right

1   other complete deficiency
Includes : left, bilateral *, and side unspecified

2   incomplete deficiency, upper third right

3   other incomplete deficiency, upper third

4   incomplete deficiency, middle third right

5   other incomplete deficiency, middle third

6   incomplete deficiency, lower third right

7   other incomplete deficiency, lower third

8   other incomplete deficiency, right
Includes : incomplete deficiency of carpus or tarsus,
right

9   other incomplete, or unspecified extent

75.0   *Transverse deficiency of shoulder* (Sh)
Includes : fore-quarter amputation
Excludes : deficiencies where only a portion of the shoulder is
missing (77)
shoulder disarticulation (75.1)

75.1   *Transverse deficiency of upper arm* (Ar)
Includes : shoulder disarticulation

75.2   *Transverse deficiency of forearm* (Fo)
Includes : elbow disarticulation

75.3   *Transverse deficiency of carpus* (Ca)
Includes : wrist disarticulation

75.4   *Transverse deficiency of pelvis* (Pel)
Includes : hind-quarter amputation

75.5   *Transverse deficiency of thigh* (Th)
Includes : hip disarticulation

75.6   *Transverse deficiency of lower leg* (Le)
Includes : knee disarticulation

75.7   *Transverse deficiency of tarsus* (Ta)
Includes : ankle disarticulation

75.8 *   *Transverse deficiencies at multiple sites in proximal parts of limbs*

75.9   *Unspecified site in proximal parts of limb*
         Includes   upper limb (UL) (transverse) deficiency
                      lower limb (LL) (transverse) deficiency
                      deficiency of hand or foot NOS

76   **Transverse deficiency of distal parts of limb**
         (see chart after category 79)
         Includes : where rays identifiable in hand or foot

         The following fourth-digit code to indicate the extent of the deficiency
         is suggested for use with this category :
         0   deficiency of all rays
         1   deficiency of first ray, complete
         2   other deficiency of first ray
         3   deficiency of second ray, complete
         4   other deficiency of second ray
         5   deficiency of third ray, complete
         6   other deficiency of third ray
         7   deficiency of fourth ray, complete
         8   other deficiency of fourth ray
         9   deficiency of fifth ray, or of unspecified ray

76.0   *Transverse deficiency of metacarpal, right* (MC)
76.1   *Other transverse deficiency of metacarpal*
76.2   *Transverse deficiency of phalanges of fingers, right* (Ph)
76.3   *Other transverse deficiency of phalanges of fingers*
76.4   *Transverse deficiency of metatarsal , right* (MT)
76.5   *Other transverse deficiency of metatarsal*
76.6   *Transverse deficiency of phalanges of toes, right* (Ph)
76.7   *Other transverse deficiency of phalanges of toes*
76.8 *   *Transverse deficiencies at multiple sites in limb*
         Includes : deficiencies at multiple sites in distal parts of limbs,
                     and mixed transverse deficiencies of proximal and
                     distal parts of limbs
76.9   *Unspecified site*

77   **Longitudinal deficiency of proximal parts of upper limb**
         (see chart after category 79)
         Includes : those of arm and carpus

The following fourth-digit subclassification to indicate the extent of the deficiency is suggested for use with this category, and also with 78

0	complete deficiency, right
1	other complete deficiency
2	incomplete deficiency, right
3	other incomplete deficiency
8	other
9	unspecified extent

77.0   *Longitudinal deficiency of scapula* (Sc)

77.1   *Longitudinal deficiency of clavicle* (Cl)

77.2   *Longitudinal deficiency of humerus* (Hu)

77.3   *Longitudinal deficiency of radius* (Ra)

77.4   *Longitudinal deficiency of ulna* (Ul)

77.5   *Longitudinal deficiency of radial elements of carpus* (Ca)

77.6   *Longitudinal deficiency of central elements of carpus*

77.7   *Longitudinal deficiency of other elements of carpus*

77.8   *Longitudinal deficiencies at multiple sites in proximal parts of upper limb*

77.9   *Unspecified site in proximal part of upper limb*
        Includes : upper limb (UL) longitudinal deficiency

78   **Longitudinal deficiency of proximal parts of lower limb**
        (see chart after category 79)
        Includes : those of leg and tarsus

        The same fourth-digit subclassification as for 77 is suggested for use with this category

78.0   *Longitudinal deficiency of ilium* (Il)

78.1   *Longitudinal deficiency of ischium* (Is)

78.2   *Longitudinal deficiency of pubis* (Pu)

78.3   *Longitudinal deficiency of femur* (Fem)

78.4   *Longitudinal deficiency of tibia* (Ti)

78.5   *Longitudinal deficiency of fibula* (Fib)

78.6   *Longitudinal deficiency of tibial elements of tarsus* (Ta)

78.7   *Longitudinal deficiency of other elements of tarsus*

78.8 * *Longitudinal deficiencies at multiple sites in proximal parts of limb*

78.9   *Unspecified site*
        Includes : lower limb (LL) longitudinal deficiency, and longitudinal deficiency NOS

79   **Longitudinal deficiency of distal parts of limb**
       (see chart on next page)
       Includes : where rays identifiable in hand or foot

       The following fourth-digit subclassification to indicate the extent of the deficiency is suggested for use with this category :

0	deficiency of all rays
1	deficiency of first ray, complete
2	other deficiency of first ray
3	deficiency of second ray, complete
4	other deficiency of second ray
5	deficiency of third ray, complete
6	other deficiency of third ray
7	deficiency of fourth ray, complete
8	other deficiency of fourth ray
9	deficiency of fifth ray, or of unspecified ray

79.0   *Longitudinal deficiency of metacarpal, right* (MC)
79.1   *Other longitudinal deficiency of metacarpal*
79.2   *Longitudinal deficiency of phalanges of fingers, right* (Ph)
79.3   *Other longitudinal deficiency of phalanges of fingers*
79.4   *Longitudinal deficiency of metatarsal , right* (MT)
79.5   *Other longitudinal deficiency of metatarsal*
79.6   *Longitudinal deficiency of phalanges of toes, right* (Ph)
79.7   *Other longitudinal deficiency of phalanges of toes*
79.8 *   *Longitudinal deficiencies at multiple sites in limbs*
79.9   *Unspecified site*

REFERENCE CHART FOR NOMENCLATURE OF DEFICIENCIES OF LIMBS

ISPO-preferred	Frantz-O'Rahilly (original)	Frantz-O'Rahilly (revised)	European	Other
TRANSVERSE DEFICIENCIES (T-)				
arm, complete	amelia, upper	amelia, upper	amelia, upper	shoulder disarticulation
thigh, complete	amelia, lower	amelia, lower	amelia, lower	hip disarticulation
arm, middle (third)	hemimelia (A/E)	meromelia, humerus M	peromelia, mid-humeral	short above-elbow stump
thigh, lower (third)	hemimelia (A/K)	meromelia, femur D	peromelia, lower femoral	long above-knee stump
forearm, complete	hemimelia (E-D)	meromelia, radio-ulnar	peromelia at level of elbow	elbow disarticulation
leg, complete	hemimelia (K-D)	meromelia, tibio-fibular	peromelia at level of knee	knee disarticulation
forearm, lower (third)	partial hemimelia	meromelia, radius D, ulna D	peromelia, lower radio-ulnar	partial aplasia of radius and ulna
leg, upper (third)	partial hemimelia	meromelia, tibia P, fibula P	peromelia, upper tibio-fibular	partial aplasia of tibia and fibula
carpal, complete	acheiria			wrist disarticulation
metacarpal, complete	adactylia			
phalanges, complete	aphalangia			
LONGITUDINAL DEFICIENCIES (L/)				
humerus, complete	proximal phocomelia			(intercalary transverse)
tibial-fibular, complete	distal phocomelia			(intercalary longitudinal)
ulnar, complete	complete paraxial hemimelia, ulnar	meromelia, ulnar	ectromelia with complete axial aplasia, ulnar	(terminal longitudinal)
radial, complete; carpal, partial; MC 1.2, complete; Ph 1.2, complete	complete paraxial hemimelia, radial	meromelia, radial	ectromelia with axial aplasia	
tibial, partial; tarsal, partial; MT 1.2, complete; Ph 1.2, complete	incomplete paraxial hemimelia, tibial	meromelia, tibial M, D	ectromelia with partial aplasia of tibia and complete aplasia of tarsals, metatarsals, and phalanges	

The above are only examples, and further details may be derived from "The proposed international terminology for the classification of congenital limb deficiencies", *Developmental medicine and child neurology.* 17, Suppl. 34 (1975) .

8 DISFIGURING IMPAIRMENTS

Disfiguring impairments include those with a potential to interfere with or otherwise disturb social relationships with other people. The concept has been interpreted broadly so as to include conditions that may not be the consequence of specific diseases, such as disfigurement, as well as disorders that may impair control of bodily functions in the manner that is customary and socially acceptable. However, more specifically biomedical impairments with a potential to engender aversion (for instance, abnormal movements of parts of the body) have been classified to one of the preceding sections

DISFIGUREMENTS OF HEAD AND TRUNK REGIONS (80-83)
Excludes : those of ear (49), of eye (58), of sexual organs (67), and of posture and physique (70)

80   Deficiency in head region

80.0   *Deficiency of cranial vault*

80.1   *Deficiency of upper jaw*

80.2   *Deficiency of lower jaw*
        Excludes : prognathism and underdevelopment of lower jaw (70.1)

80.3   *Other deficiency of skull*

80.4   *Cleft palate*

80.5   *Other dentofacial deficiency*

80.6   *Deficiency of nose*

80.8   *Other*

80.9   *Unspecified*

81   Structural deformity in head and trunk regions

81.0   *Deformity of nose*

81.1   *Deformity of head shape*
        Includes : hydrocephaly, microcephaly, and abnormality of skull shape

81.2   *Accessory structures in head region*

81.3   *Other deformity of head region*
        Includes : lips, tongue, and palate

81.4   *Deficiency in neck region*
        Excludes : deficiency of vertebra (70.51)

81.5   *Deficiency in thorax*
        Excludes : internal organs (65)

81.6   *Deficiency in abdominal wall*

81.7   *Other deficiency in abdomen*
        Excludes : internal organs (65)

81.8   *Other*
        Includes : funnel chest

81.9   *Unspecified*

82   Other disfigurement of head
        Includes : face

82.0   *Other soft tissue deficiency of head*
        Includes : wasting

82.1   *Swelling of part of head*
        Includes : tumours

82.2   *Pigmentation of skin of head*
        Includes : depigmentation

82.3   *Other colour changes of head*
        Includes : cyanosis, flushing, rashes, and skin infections

82.4   *Baldness, partial or complete*

82.5   *Other abnormality of hair*

82.6   *Scarring of head*

82.7   *Other abnormality of skin of head*

82.8   *Other disfigurement of head*
        Includes : marked ugliness (e.g., gargoylism)
        Excludes : deformity of nose (81.0), dentofacial deficiencies
                    (80.4 and 80.5), and deformity of head shape (81.1)

82.9   *Unspecified*

83   Other disfigurement of trunk

83.0   *Other soft tissue deficiency of trunk*
        Includes : wasting

83.1   *Swelling of trunk*
        Includes : tumours
        Excludes : hypertrophy of breasts (67.1)

83.2   *Pigmentation of skin of trunk*
        Includes : depigmentation

83.3   *Other colour changes of trunk*
        Includes : rashes and skin infections

83.4   *Abnormal hair on trunk*

83.5   *Scarring of trunk*

83.6   *Other abnormality of skin of trunk*
Excludes : absence of nipples (67.0)

83.7   *Accessory structures on trunk*
Excludes : accessory nipples (67.2)

83.8   *Other disfigurement of trunk*

83.9   *Unspecified*

DISFIGUREMENTS OF LIMBS (84-87)

Excludes : limb deficiencies (76-79)

The following fourth-digit subclassification to indicate the location of limb disfigurements is suggested for use with categories 84-87

0   shoulder and upper arm

1   elbow and forearm

2   wrist and carpus
Excludes : disfigurement also involving the hand (3, below)

3   metacarpus and hand
Includes : disfigurement also involving wrist and carpus

4   finger
Includes : thumb
Excludes: disfigurements classifiable under 3 (above)

5   hip and thigh

6   knee and leg

7   ankle, foot, and toe

8*   multiple
Includes :   those affecting whole of limb or affecting both
             upper and lower limbs

9   location unspecified

84   Failure of differentiation of parts
Includes : failure of separation of parts

84.0   *Congenital deformity*
84.1   *Synostosis*

84.2   *Congenital soft-tissue contracture*
        Includes : contracture secondary to failure of differentiation of
                muscle, ligament, and capsular structures, such as
                arthrogryposis, camptodactyly, and trigger digit
84.3   *Congenital skeletal contracture*
        Includes : clinodactyly

84.4   *Simple syndactylia*
84.5   *Soft-tissue syndactylia*
        Includes : synonychia
84.6   *Skeletal syndactylia*
        Includes : fusions, acrosyndactylia, Apert's syndrome, and
                brachysyndactylia
84.8   *Other*
84.9   *Unspecified*

85   **Other congenital malformation**
        Excludes : those of internal organs (65 and 66)

85.0   *Hypoplasia of skin and nails*
85.1   *Hypoplasia of musculotendinous structures*
85.2   *Hypoplasia of neurovascular structures*
85.3   *Other hypoplasia*
        Includes : hypoplasia of more than one of preceding types of
                tissue (85.0-85.2)
        Excludes : dwarfism (70.60), and achondroplasia and generalized
                skeletal defect (70.65)
85.4   *Overgrowth*
        Excludes : impairment of physique and gigantism (70.61)
85.5   *Skeletal duplications*
        Includes : those of bones of limbs
85.6   *Other duplications*
        Includes : those of all tissues, such as polydactylism and mirror
                hand
85.7   *Congenital constriction band*
85.8   *Other*
        Includes : arachnodactyly
85.9   *Unspecified*

86   **Other structural disfigurement**

86.0   *Wasting, complete*
        Excludes : emaciation (70.63)

86.1   *Other wasting*
86.2   *Other soft-tissue deficiency, complete*
86.3   *Other soft-tissue deficiency*
86.4   *Swelling of tissues*
         Includes : tumours
         Excludes : that due to fluid (86.5 and 86.6)
86.5   *Other swelling, complete*
         Includes : lymphoedema
86.6   *Other swelling*
         Includes : oedema
86.7   *Accessory structures*
         Excludes : accessory digits (85.6)
86.8   *Other structural disfigurement*
86.9   *Unspecified*

87   Other disfigurement

87.0   *Pigmentation*
         Includes : depigmentation
87.1   *Cyanosis*
87.2   *Other disturbance of skin colouration*
         Includes : bruising, rashes, and skin infections
         Excludes : generalized bruising (92.4)
87.3   *Other circulatory disturbance of skin*
         Includes : varicose veins
87.4   *Disturbance of sweating*
87.5   *Exudation*
         Includes : scaling
87.6   *Scarring*
87.7   *Abnormal hair*
87.8   *Other abnormality of skin*
87.9   *Other and unspecified*

OTHER DISFIGURING IMPAIRMENTS (88-89)

88   Abnormal orifice

88.0   *Tracheostomy*
88.1   *Gastrostomy*
88.2   *Ileostomy*

88.3 *Colostomy*

88.4 *Other gastrointestinal diversion*

88.5 *Indwelling urinary catheter*

88.6 *Other urinary diversion*
Includes : extraurethral incontinence

88.7 *Other artificial orifice*

88.8 *Other abnormal orifice*

88.9 *Unspecified*

89 Other disfiguring impairment

9   GENERALIZED, SENSORY, AND OTHER IMPAIRMENTS

GENERALIZED IMPAIRMENTS (90-94)

90   **Multiple impairment**

90.0*   *Multiple, of all classes*

90.1*   *Multiple, of mental functions, speech, and special senses*
Includes :   if with viscera or with skeleton

90.2*   *Multiple, of mental functions and speech*

90.3*   *Multiple, of special senses, viscera, and skeleton*

90.4*   *Multiple, of special senses*

90.5*   *Multiple, of viscera and skeleton*

90.8*   *Other*

90.9*   *Unspecified*

91   **Severe impairment of continence**
Excludes :   reflex, overflow, urge, and stress incontinence (63)

91.0   *Subject to control by devices*
Includes :   adaptive devices and electrical stimulators
Excludes :   special protective clothing (classify appropriately to 91.1-91.8)

91.1   *Double incontinence with frequency greater than once every night and once every day*
Includes :   soiling (faecal incontinence) and wetting (incontinence of urine) greater than specified frequencies

91.2   *Other double incontinence every night and every day*

91.3   *Double incontinence with frequency greater than once every week by night and by day*

91.4   *Other double incontinence*

91.5   *Faecal incontinence with frequency greater than once every 24 hours*

91.6   *Other faecal incontinence with frequency greater than once every week*

91.7   *Incontinence of urine with frequency greater than once every 24 hours*

91.8   *Other*

91.9   *Unspecified*
Excludes :   faecal incontinence NOS (62.9)

92   Undue susceptibility to trauma
Excludes : intermittent impairment of consciousness (21) and impairment of balance function (48)

92.0   *Haemorrhagic disorders*
Includes : bleeding tendencies
Excludes : bruising (92.4)

92.1   *Skeletal fragility*

92.2   *Other undue susceptibility to fracture*

92.3   *Undue susceptibility to pressure sores*

92.4   *Generalized bruising*

92.5   *Undue insensitivity to pain*

92.6   *Other undue susceptibility of tissues*
Includes : scurvy

92.7   *Reduced recuperative powers associated with ageing*

92.8   *Other*

92.9   *Unspecified*

93   Metabolic impairment
Excludes : impairment of physique (70.6) and skeletal fragility (92.1)

93.0   *Impairment of growth*
Includes : failure to thrive and failure of maturation

93.1   *Delicate*

93.2   *Specific dietary intolerance*
Includes : gluten sensitivity

93.3   *Other dietary limitation*
Includes : diabetes
Excludes : food intolerance (62.0)

93.4   *Malnutrition*

93.5   *Weight loss*
Excludes : emaciation (70.63)

93.6   *Weight gain*
Excludes : obesity (70.64)

93.7   *Polydipsia*

93.8   *Other*

93.9   *Unspecified*

94   Other generalized impairment
Excludes : impairment of sleep (22)

94.0   *Subject to electromechanical devices for life support*
Includes : pacemaker, renal dialysis, and respirator

94.1   *Intermittent prostration*
Includes : such as may occur with asthma or migraine
Excludes : vertigo (48.0)

94.2   *Generalized pain*

94.3   *Fever*
Includes : pyrexia

94.4   *Generalized pruritus*

94.5   *Other weakness*
Includes : (generalized) weakness NOS

94.6   *Generalized fatigue*
Includes : fatigue NOS
Excludes : fatigability (28.5)

94.8   *Other*

94.9   *Unspecified*

SENSORY IMPAIRMENTS (95-98)

95   Sensory impairment of head

95.0   *Anaesthesia*
Excludes : anaesthetic eye (58.2)

95.1   *Disturbance of sweating*

95.2   *Temperature change*

95.3   *Facial pain*

95.4   *Headache*

95.5   *Other ache in head*
Includes : congestion, throbbing, and tightness
Excludes : earache (49.3)

95.6   *Itching*

95.7   *Numbness*
Includes : paraesthesia and tingling

95.8   *Other*

95.9   *Unspecified*

96   Sensory impairment of trunk

96.0   *Anaesthesia*

96.1 *Disturbance of sweating*

96.2 *Temperature change*

96.3 *Back pain*
Includes : neck pain and lumbago

96.4 *Other pain in trunk region*
Excludes : abdominal pain (62.3), chest pain (61.3 and 61.4), and renal colic (63.0)

96.5 *Other ache in trunk region*
Includes : congestion and tightness
Excludes : chest pain (61.3 and 61.4) and tightness of chest related to exercise (61.5)

96.6 *Itching*

96.7 *Numbness*
Includes : paraesthesia and tingling

96.8 *Other*

96.9 *Unspecified*

97 Sensory impairment of upper limb

97.0 *Anaesthesia*

97.1 *Disturbance of deep sensibility*
Includes : astereognosis

97.2 *Temperature change*

97.3 *Pain on exercise*

97.4 *Other pain*
Includes : causalgia

97.5 *Other ache*
Includes : congestion and tightness

97.6 *Itching*

97.7 *Numbness*
Includes : paraesthesia and tingling

97.8 *Other*
Includes : burning or prickling, and cramp or spasm

97.9 *Unspecified*

98 Other sensory impairment
Includes : that of lower limb

98.0 *Anaesthesia*

98.1   *Disturbance of deep sensibility*
        Includes : astereognosis

98.2   *Temperature change*

98.3   *Pain*
        Includes : causalgia
        Excludes : pain on exercise (61.5)

98.4   *Other ache*
        Includes : congestion or tightness
        Excludes : intermittent claudication (61.5)

98.5   *Itching*
        Excludes : generalized pruritus (94.4)

98.6   *Numbness*
        Includes : paraesthesia and tingling

98.8   *Other*
        Includes : burning or prickling, and cramp or spasm

98.9   *Unspecified*

OTHER IMPAIRMENTS (99)

99   Other impairment

99.0   *Currently pregnant*
        (Pregnancy has been included within this classification
        because it is associated with certain functional limitations)

99.1   *Gangrene of upper limb*

99.2   *Gangrene of lower limb*

99.3   *Other gangrene*
        Includes : that affecting upper and lower limb

99.8   *Other*

99.9   *Unspecified*
        Includes : impairment NOS

GUIDANCE ON ASSIGNMENT

Impairments resemble disease terms in the ICD in that they are best conceived of as threshold phenomena ; for any particular category, all that is involved is a judgement about whether the impairment is present or not.

The apparent comprehensiveness of the code may at first appear to be daunting. However, the level of detail provided serves two purposes : first, as a means of defining the content of classes, and, secondly, to allow for considerable specificity for users who may wish to record such detail. The taxonomic structure of the code resembles that of the ICD in that it is hierarchical, with meaning preserved even if the code is used only in abbreviated form. Thus the level of detail to be recorded is a matter of choice for the user.

Hitherto, the more immediate consequences of disease — the major impairments — are generally likely to have been noted in records. Thus coding to appropriate categories of the I code of whatever has been recorded should not present insuperable difficulties. The principal problem is likely to be concerned with under-ascertainment — the degree to which significant impairments may not have been noted.

From now on, it is suggested that the nine major sections of the I code be used as a check-list that is applied to each individual. This would require that the observer ask himself a series of questions : "Does this person have an intellectual impairment, does he have any other psychological impairment, does he have a language impairment ?" and so on, in sequence. Further information on any questions answered affirmatively, along the lines of the greater detail contained in the code, could then be elicited.

The main aspect likely to command attention in the future relates to identification criteria and their relation to severity. The difficulties have been noted under "Deviation from norms", in the earlier section on the *Consequences of disease.*

ALPHABETICAL INDEX

In the alphabetical list below, the code numbers of impairments may be of two, three or four digits, e.g., Deaf mutism 40, Tunnel vision 56.6, Kyphosis 70.50. A dash (–) may replace the fourth digit, e.g., Paralysis, limb(s) NEC 73.9–; this means that fourth-digit subdivisions exist but have not been indexed and that the coder should refer to the classification of impairments itself in order to assign the appropriate fourth digit. In the above example, the coder would find on page 97 a fourth-digit subclassification for rubrics 73.0 to 73.9 indicating the nature of the paralysis.

A

Abdominal pain 62.3

Abnormal, abnormality, abnormally
– activity during sleep 22.5
– blood vessels of thorax and abdomen 66.0
– hair (head) NEC 82.5
– – limb (lower) (upper) 87.7-
– – trunk 83.4
– limited gesture 33.3
– muscle tension 33.3
– quiet voice 36.3
– rapid speech 37.1
– skin NEC
– – head 82.7
– – limb (lower) (upper) 87.8-
– – trunk 83.6
– skull shape 81.1
– sleep/wakefulness pattern 22.3
– sounds in chest 61.2
– tissues in trunk region NEC 70.72
– viscera, structural NEC 66.4

Absence
– eye NEC 50.9
– – both 50.0
– – one, visual impairment of other eye
– – – moderate 50.5
– – – near-total 50.2
– – – none 50.7
– – – profound 50.3
– – – severe 50.4
– – – slight 50.6
– – – total 50.1
– – – unspecified 50.8
– limb (total) - see Deficiency, transverse
– nipples 67.0
Acalculia 19.2
Acceleration of thought 17.3

Accessory
– digits 85.6-
– structures
– – head (region) 81.2
– – limb (lower) (upper) 86.7-
– – trunk 83.7
– viscera 66.3
Ache (lower limb) NEC 98.4
– head 95.4
– trunk (region) 96.5
– upper limb 97.5
Achondroplasia 70.65
Acrosyndactylia 84.6-
Acts, impulsive 27.7
Addiction, drug 25.6
Agenesis, limb - see Deficiency, transverse
Aggressivity 29.7
Agitation 33.3
Agnosia 19.0
Agoraphobia 29.6
Alcohol dependence 25.5
Alcoholism 25.5
Alienation (parts) of own body 23.30
Ambiguity, sexual 64.4
Ambitendence 27.4
Ambivalence of affect 26.7
Amblyopia 57.7
Amelia - see Deficiency, longitudinal
Amnesia NEC (for) 15.9
– congrade 15.2
– figures 15.6
– long-term events 15.1
– psychogenic 15.3
– recent events 15.2
– retrograde 15.0
– shapes 15.4
– specified type NEC 15.8
– words 15.5

Amputation (stump), limb - *see* Deficiency, transverse
Anesthesia (limb) NEC   98.0
- eye   58.2
- head NEC   95.0
- lower limb   98.0
- trunk   96.0
- upper limb   97.0
Anesthetic eye   58.2
Aneurysm, aortic   66.0
Angry outbursts   26.5
Anhedonia   26.1
Ankylosis, limb, NEC - *see* categories 71.0-71.7 with 4th digit 1
- bilateral - *see* categories 71.0-71.7 with 4th digit 0
Anomalies of cardiac development   65.21
Anorexia   25.0
Anosognosia   19.0
Anxiety NEC   26.09
- free-floating   26.00
- pathological   26.00

Anxiety NEC - *continued*
- phobic   26.01
- specified type NEC   26.08
Aortic aneurysm   66.0
Apathy   26.2
Apert's syndrome   84.6-
Appetite
- decreased   25.0
- increased   25.1
Apraxia   19.1
Arachnodactyly   85.8-
Arrhythmia   61.6
Arthrogryposis   84.2-
Artificial larynx   35.0
Astereognosis (lower limb)   98.1
- upper limb   97.1
Astigmatism   57.1
Attacks, panic   26.01
Attempted control of affect display   26.81
Attention-seeking   29.84
Autism   30.1
Automatic bladder   63.3
Awakening premature from sleep   22.1

B

Baldness (complete) (partial)   82.4
Banging head   29.82
Behavior, solitary   29.85
Biliary colic   62.3
Blank spells   24.4
Bleeding
- rectal   62.8
- tendencies   92.0
- vaginal   64.6
Blepharitis   58.5
Blindness (bilateral) NEC   51.9
- one eye NEC   54.9
- - with low vision of other eye   52.9

Blunting of affect   26.2
Blurred vision   58.7
Borborygmi   62.2
Brachysyndactylia   84.6-
Bruising - *see also* Color changes
- generalized   92.4
Bulimia   25.1
Burning sensation (lower limb)   98.8
- upper limb   97.8

C

Camptodactyly   84.2-
Cardiac murmurs   61.2
Caries (teeth)   68.2
Catastrophic reaction   26.80
Catatonic movements   33.3
Causalgia (lower limb)   98.3
- upper limb   97.4
Chilblains (lower limb) (upper limb)   87.3-
Circumstantial thinking   17.5

Claudication, intermittent   61.5
Cleft palate   80.4
Clicking jaw   70.15
Clinodactyly   84.3-
Clouding of consciousness   20.1
Colic
- biliary   62.3
- intestinal   62.3
- renal   63.0

Color changes NEC
- head 82.3
- limb (lower) (upper) 87.2-
- trunk 83.3
Colostomy 88.3
Coma 20.0
Compulsion(s) 27.5
- repetition 29.5
Confabulation 16.0
Confusion 20.4
Congestion - *see also* Ache
- head 95.5
Constipation 62.4
Constriction band, congenital 85.7-

Contraceptive procedure in use 64.0
Contracted pelvis 70.70
Contracture, congenital
- skeletal 84.3-
- soft tissue 84.2-
Cough 61.7
Cramp (lower limb) 98.8
- upper limb 97.8
Craving, pathological (alcohol) (drug) 25.7
Cryptomnesia 16.2
Curvature, spinal 70.50
Cyanosis
- head 82.3
- limb (lower) (upper) 87.1-

D

Deaf mutism 40
Deafness (bilateral) (*see also* Loss, hearing, total) 41.9
- one ear 44.9
- psychogenic 43.9
Decay (teeth) 68.2
Decreased
- appetite 25.0
- libido 25.3
Deficiency
- abdomen 81.7
- - wall 81.6
- all rays - *see* categories 76- & 79- with 4th digit 0
- bladder 65.7
- cranial vault 80.0
- dentofacial NEC 80.5
- ear NEC 49.9
- - external 49.7
- - inner 49.0
- - middle 49.5
- esophagus 65.3
- eyelid 58.5
- fifth ray NEC - *see* categories 76- & 79- with 4th digit 9
- first ray NEC - *see* categories 76- & 79- with 4th digit 2
- - complete - *see* categories 76- & 79- with 4th digit 1
- foot NEC 75.9-
- fourth ray NEC - *see* categories 76- & 79- with 4th digit 8
- - complete - *see* categories 76- & 79- with 4th digit 7
- gall bladder 65.5
- genitalia

Deficiency - *continued*
- genitalia - *continued*
- - external 67.6
- - internal 65.8
- hand NEC 75.9-
- head (region) NEC 80.9
- - specified part NEC 80.8
- heart NEC 65.29
- - specified type NEC 65.28
- - subject to corrective or prosthetic intervention 65.20
- internal organs NEC 65.9
- intestine 65.4
- kidney NEC 65.69
- - specified type NEC 65.68
- - subject to renal transplantation 65.60
- larynx 35.1
- liver 65.5
- longitudinal (intercalary) (terminal) NEC 78.9-
- - distal parts of limb NEC 79.9-
- - - metacarpal NEC 79.1-
- - - - right 79.0-
- - - metatarsal NEC 79.5-
- - - - right 79.4-
- - - multiple sites 79.8-
- - - phalanx
- - - - finger NEC 79.3-
- - - - - right 79.2-
- - - - toe NEC 79.7-
- - - - - right 79.6-
- - proximal parts of limb (lower) NEC 78.9-
- - - carpus NEC 77.7-
- - - - central elements 77.6-
- - - - radial elements 77.5-

Deficiency - *continued*
- longitudinal - *continued*
- - proximal parts of limb - *continued*
- - - clavicle   77.1-
- - - complete NEC - *see* categories 77-
  & 78- with 4th digit 1
- - - - right - *see* categories 77- & 78-
  with 4th digit 0
- - - femur   78.3-
- - - fibula   78.5-
- - - humerus   77.2-
- - - ilium   78.0-
- - - incomplete NEC - *see* categories 77-
  & 78- with 4th digit 3
- - - - right - *see* categories 77- & 78-
  with 4th digit 2
- - - ischium   78.1-
- - - multiple sites   78.8-
- - - pubis   78.2-
- - - radius   77.3-
- - - scapula   77.0-
- - - tarsus NEC   78.7-
- - - - tibial elements   78.6-
- - - tibia   78.4-
- - - ulna   77.4-
- - - unspecified extent - *see* categories
  77- & 78- with 4th digit 9
- - - upper NEC   77.9-
- - - - multiple sites   77.8-
- lower
- - jaw   80.2
- - limb (transverse) NEC   75.9-
- lung   65.1
- neck (region)   81.4
- nose   80.6
- rectum   65.4
- second ray NEC - *see* categories 76- &
  79- with 4th digit 4
- - complete - *see* categories 76- & 79-
  with 4th digit 3
- skull NEC   80.3
- soft tissue
- - head NEC   82.0
- - limb (lower) (upper) NEC   86.3-
- - - complete   86.2-
- - trunk NEC   83.0
- spine NEC   70.52
- spleen   65.5
- stomach   65.3
- teeth NEC   68.2
- - complete   68.1
- third ray NEC - *see* categories 76- & 79-
  with 4th digit 6
- - complete - *see* categories 76- & 79-
  with 4th digit 5
- thorax   81.5
- tracheobronchial tree   65.0

Deficiency - *continued*
- transverse (terminal) NEC   76.9-
- - distal parts of limb NEC   76.9-
- - - metacarpal NEC   76.1-
- - - - right   76.0-
- - - metatarsal NEC   76.5-
- - - - right   76.4-
- - - multiple sites   76.8-
- - - phalanx
- - - - finger NEC   76.3-
- - - - - right   76.2-
- - - - toe NEC   76.7-
- - - - - right   76.6-
- - intercalary - *see* Deficiency,
  longitudinal
- - - and proximal parts   76.8-
- - proximal parts of limb NEC   75.9-
- - - and distal parts   76.8-
- - - carpus   75.3-
- - - complete NEC - *see* categories
  75.0-75.9 with 4th digit 1
- - - - right - *see* categories 75.0-75.9
  with 4th digit 0
- - - forearm   75.2-
- - - incomplete NEC - *see* categories
  75.0-75.9 with 4th digit 9
- - - - right NEC - *see* categories
  75.0-75.9 with 4th digit 8
- - - - lower third NEC - *see* categories
  75.0-75.9 with 4th digit 7
- - - - - right - *see* categories 75.0-75.9
  with 4th digit 6
- - - - middle third NEC - *see* categories
  75.0-75.9 with 4th digit 5
- - - - - right - *see* categories 75.0-75.9
  with 4th digit 4
- - - - upper third NEC - *see* categories
  75.0-75.9 with 4th digit 3
- - - - - right - *see* categories 75.0-75.9
  with 4th digit 2
- - - lower leg   75.6-
- - - multiple sites   75.8-
- - - pelvis   75.4-
- - - shoulder   75.0-
- - - tarsus   75.7-
- - - thigh   75.5-
- - - upper arm   75.1-
- unspecified ray - *see* categories 76- & 79-
  with 4th digit 9
- upper
- - jaw   80.1
- - limb (transverse) NEC   75.9-
- valvular, due to acquired lesions   65.22
- vertebra   70.51
Deformity (structural)
- congenital, limb (lower) (upper)   84.0-
- ear NEC   49.9

Deformity - *continued*
- ear NEC - *continued*
- - external 49.7
- - inner 49.1
- - middle 49.6
- external genitalia 67.6
- eyeball 58.4
- eyelid 58.5
- head (region) NEC 81.3
- - shape 81.1
- limb, NEC - *see* categories 71.0-71.7 with 4th digit 5
- - with fixation - *see* categories 71.0-71.7 with 4th digit 1
- - bilateral - *see* categories 71.0-71.7 with 4th digit 4
- - - with fixation - *see* categories 71.0-71.7 with 4th digit 0
- nose 81.0
- spinal NEC 70.53
- trunk (region) NEC 81.9
- - specified part NEC 81.8
"Déjà vécu" experience 23.31
"Déjà vu" experience 23.31
Delayed language comprehension and use for
- auditory stimuli 34.0
- visual stimuli 34.1
Delicate 93.1
Delirium 20.3
Delusional jealousy 18.4
Delusions (of) NEC 18.8
- depressive 18.3
- fantastic 18.6
- grandeur 18.5
- guilt 18.3
- hypochondriacal 18.7
- impoverishment 18.3
- jealousy 18.4
- nihilistic 18.7
- paranoid 18.2
- reference 18.2
Dementia NEC 14.2
- global 14.0
- lacunar 14.1
- patchy 14.1
Dental prosthesis in use 68.0
Dependence (on)
- alcohol 25.5
- drug 25.6
- life support devices 94.0
- pacemaker 94.0
- renal dialysis 94.0
- respirator 94.0
Depersonalization 23.30
Depigmentation - *see* Pigmentation
Depression 26.1

Derealization 23.31
Dermatitis, ear 49.3
Destructiveness NEC 29.83
Diabetes 93.3
Dialysis (renal) 94.0
Diaphragmatic palsy 60.4
Diarrhea 62.5
Dietary
- intolerance 93.2
- limitation 93.3
Difficulty (in)
- getting off to sleep 22.0
- reading 34.2
- specific learning NEC 34.5
- understanding language (spoken) (written) 34.5
- using language (spoken) (written) 34.5
Diplopia 57.3
Disarticulation
- ankle 75.7-
- elbow 75.2-
- hip 75.5-
- knee 75.6-
- shoulder 75.1-
- wrist 75.3-
Discharge
- aural 49.2
- genital 67.3
- nasal 69.3
- ocular 58.0
- urethral 67.3
- vaginal 67.3
Disfigurement NEC 89
- external ear 49.7
- eyeball 58.4
- eyelid 58.5
- face NEC 82.9
- - specified type NEC 82.8
- head NEC 82.9
- - specified type NEC 82.8
- limb (lower) (upper) NEC 87.9-
- - ankle, foot and toe - *see* categories 84-87 with 4th digit 7
- - elbow and forearm - *see* categories 84-87 with 4th digit 1
- - finger - *see* categories 84-87 with 4th digit 4
- - hip and thigh - *see* categories 84-87 with 4th digit 5
- - knee and leg - *see* categories 84-87 with 4th digit 6
- - metacarpus and hand - *see* categories 84-87 with 4th digit 3
- - multiple - *see* categories 84-87 with 4th digit 8
- - shoulder and upper arm - *see* categories 84-87 with 4th digit 0

Disfigurement NEC - *continued*
- limb - *continued*

– – structural NEC 86.9-
– – – specified type NEC 86.8-
– – unspecified - *see* categories 84-87 with
  4th digit 9
– – wrist and carpus - *see* categories 84-87
  with 4th digit 2
– trunk NEC 83.9
– – specified type NEC 83.8

Dislocation, limbs - *see* categories 71.0-71.7
  with 4th digit 7

Disorder (of)
– body image 23.32
– central
– – visual function NEC 31.2
– – – and speech, with severe impairment
  of communication 30.1
– – – with inability to communicate 31.0
– heart valves, acquired 65.22
– hemorrhagic 92.0

Disorientation (time, place, persons) 20.4

Dissociative state 20.5

Distortion (of)
– memory content NEC 16.3
– perception NEC 23.19
– – specified type NEC 23.18
– visual 57.7

Distractibility 24.0

Distress NEC 26.85

Disturbance
– attention NEC 24.9
– – intensity 24.0
– – mobility 24.3
– – span 24.2
– body awareness NEC 23.39
– – specified type NEC 23.38
– breathing 61.1
– cardiac rhythm 61.6
– circulatory, skin of limb (lower) (upper)
  87.3-
– consciousness, intermittent 21.4
– deep sensibility (lower limb) 98.1
– – upper limb 97.1
– facial expression NEC 70.23
– feelings NEC 26.9
– jaw development NEC 70.14
– menstrual function NEC 64.8
– perception NEC 23.19
– – body image 23.32
– – time and space 23.4

Disturbance - *continued*
– sexual
– – functions NEC (with normal libido)
  25.49
– – – specified type NEC 25.48
– – performance NEC (with normal
  libido) 25.49
– – – specified type NEC 25.48
– sweating
– – head 95.1
– – limb (lower) (upper) 87.4-
– – trunk 96.1
– time and space perception 23.4

Diversion
– gastrointestinal NEC 88.4
– urinary NEC 88.6

Dizziness 48.0

Drawling (speech) 35.5

Drop-attacks 21.6

Drug
– addiction 25.6
– dependence 25.6

Dry
– eye 58.3
– mouth 68.4

Dulling of perception
– selective 23.01
– specific modalities 23.01
– uniform 23.00

Dumping syndrome 62.7

Duplications NEC
– limb (tissues) 85.6-
– skeletal (bones of limbs) 85.5-
– viscera 66.3

Dwarfism 70.60

Dysarthria NEC 35.4
– severe 35.3

Dysfunction, jaw NEC 70.15

Dyskinesia 70.54

Dyslexia NEC 31.1
– severe 31.0

Dysmenorrhea 64.5

Dyspareunia 64.3

Dysphasia NEC 30.3
– severe 30.2

Dyspnea 61.0

Dystonia 70.54

Dysuria 63.7

E

Ectromelia - *see* Deficiency, longitudinal
Edema, limb (lower) (upper) 86.6-
Edentulous 68.1
Ejaculatio praecox 25.41
Elation 26.4
Emaciation 70.63
Emotional
 - immaturity 26.84
 - lability 26.6
Enuresis nocturna 22.4
Epilepsy NEC 21.5
 - with frequency of seizures
 - - less than once per month 21.3
 - - once per
 - - - day or greater 21.0
 - - - month or greater 21.2
 - - - week or greater 21.1
 - psychomotor 21.4

Epistaxis 69.3
Eructation 62.2
Euphoria 26.4
Eversion, eyelid 58.5
Excessive
 - sensitivity 29.2
 - shyness 29.2
 - sleeping 22.2
 - vulnerability 29.2
Excitement NEC 26.4
 - gross 26.3
 - psychomotor 28.2
Exophthalmos 58.4
Expressionless voice 36.1
Exudation, limb (lower) (upper) 87.5-

F

Facial
 - involuntary movements 70.21
 - mannerisms 70.22
 - palsy 70.20
 - paralysis 70.20
Failure (of) (to)
 - differentiation of parts NEC 84.9-
 - - specified type NEC 84.8-
 - maturation 93.0
 - renal 63.1
 - respiratory 61.0
 - thrive 93.0
False perception 23.29
 - specified type NEC 23.28
Fatigability 28.5
Fatigue (generalized) NEC 94.6
 - limbs - *see* categories 73.0-73.9 with 4th
   digit 7
Fecal incontinence NEC 62.9
 - frequency greater than once every
 - - week 91.6
 - - 24 hours 91.5
Feeble-minded 13.0
Feeling of guilt 26.83
Fever 94.3
Fixation, limb, NEC - *see* categories
   71.0-71.7 with 4th digit 1
 - bilateral - *see* categories 71.0-71.7 with
   4th digit 0

Fixed attention 24.3
Flail joint - *see* categories 71.0-71.7 with
   4th digit 3
 - bilateral - *see* categories 71.0-71.7 with
   4th digit 2
Flatulence 62.2
Flight of ideas 17.7
Floaters 57.7
Flushing - *see* Color changes
Food intolerance 62.0
Forequarter amputation 75.0-
Forgetfulness 16.4
Fragility, skeletal 92.1
Free-floating anxiety 26.00
Frequency of micturition 63.2
Frigidity 25.42
Fugue states 21.7
Funnel chest 81.8

G

Gangrene NEC (lower and upper limb)
  99.3
- lower limb 99.2
- upper limb 99.1
Gargoylism 82.8

Gastrostomy 88.1
Gigantism 70.61
Gluten sensitivity 93.2
Grand mal (*see also* Epilepsy) 21.5
Guilt feeling 26.83

H

Hallucination NEC 23.25
- auditory 23.21
- gustatory 23.24
- olfactory 23.23
- tactile 23.22
- visual 23.20
Hallucinatory state (oneroid) (dream-like)
  23.27
Hard of hearing (*see also* Impairment,
  hearing) NEC 43.9
- bilateral 43.8
Headache 95.4
Heart block 61.6
Heightening of perception (uniform) 23.02
- selective 23.03
Hemianopia 56.7
Hemiballismus 74.50
Hemimelia - *see* Deficiency, longitudinal
Hemiparesis (spastic) 72.2
Hemiplegia (spastic) NEC 72.1
- dominant side 72.0
- with speech involvement 72.0
Hemoptysis 61.8

Hemorrhage, internal (organs) 66.1
Hemorrhoids 62.8
Hermaphroditism 64.4
Hiccough 62.2
Hindquarter amputation 75.4-
Histrionic traits 29.80
Hostility 29.7
Hydrocephaly 81.1
Hyperkinesia in children 28.3
Hypermotility gastrointestinal 62.7
Hyperorexia 25.1
Hypersensitivity to noise 23.03
Hypersomnia 22.2
Hypertrophy, breasts 67.1
Hypnotic state 20.6
Hypoactivity 28.1
Hypochondriasis 29.3
Hypomania 26.4
Hypoplasia NEC 85.3-
- musculotendinous structures 85.1-
- neurovascular structures 85.2-
- skin and nails 85.0-
Hypospadias 67.6

I

IQ
- less than 20 10
- 20-34 11
- 35-49 12
- 50-70 13.0
Idiosyncratic
- patterns of body movement 33.3
- speech 38.0
Idiot 10
Ileostomy 88.2
Illusions NEC 23.14
- acoustic 23.11
- composite 23.15

Illusions NEC - *continued*
- kinesthetic 23.13
- memory 16.1
- optical 23.10
- specified sense modalities NEC 23.14
- tactile 23.12
Imbecile 12
Imitation (sounds) 32.0
Immaturity, emotional 26.84
Immobility of face 28.1
Impairment (of) NEC 99.9
- ability to
- - acquire new information 15.2

Impairment - *continued*
- ability to - *continued*
- - mix with people   29.2
- - shift focus of attention   24.3
- abstraction   17.0
- affect NEC   26.9
- - specified type NEC   26.88
- alertness   24.6
- attention NEC   24.9
- - specified type NEC   24.8
- auditory
- - function NEC   47.9
- - - mixed types   47.4
- - - specified type NEC   47.8
- - sensitivity NEC   45.9
- aural function NEC   49.9
- awareness   22.8
- balance   48.9
- - and vestibular functions NEC   48.9
- - - specified type NEC   48.8
- - specified type NEC   48.7
- behavior pattern NEC   29.9
- - specified type NEC   29.88
- binocular vision NEC   57.4
- body language NEC   33.3
- breasts NEC   67.2
- cardiorespiratory function NEC   61.9
- - specified type NEC   61.8
- cerebellar function NEC   48.3
- - locomotion   48.2
- clarity of consciousness NEC   20.9
- - specified type NEC   20.8
- cognitive functions (all)   14.0
- - global   14.0
- - lacunar   14.1
- - patchy   14.1
- coherence   37.5
- color vision   57.5
- communication NEC   30.9
- - severe NEC   30.5
- - - due to cerebral damage   30.4
- - - functional   30.0
- - - with central disorders of speech and
    visual function   30.1
- - total NEC   30.5
- concentration   24.1
- conceptualization   17.0
- consciousness NEC   22.9
- - specified type NEC   22.8
- continence, severe NEC   91.9
- - specified type NEC   91.8
- conversational form NEC   37.7
- coordinating function   48.3
- development of hearing, total or
    profound   40
- dexterity NEC - *see* categories 74.0-74.9
    with 4th digit 6

Impairment - *continued*
- disfiguring NEC   89
- drives NEC   25.9
- - specified type NEC   25.88
- emotion NEC   26.9
- - specified type NEC   26.88
- external ear NEC   49.8
- extralinguistic function   32.0
- - and sublinguistic NEC   32.9
- eyelid NEC   58.6
- facial expression NEC   33.2
- flow and form of thought processes NEC
    17.9
- - specified type NEC   17.8
- gastrointestinal function NEC   62.9
- - specified type NEC   62.8
- generalized NEC   94.9
- - specified type NEC   94.8
- genitalia NEC   67.9
- - external NEC   67.7
- - internal NEC   66.5
- gnosis function   19.0
- growth   93.0
- head (region) NEC   70.9
- - specified type NEC   70.8
- hearing NEC   45.9
- - bilateral NEC   43.9
- - mild
- - - bilateral   45.7
- - - one ear
- - - - hearing impairment, other ear
- - - - - moderate   45.5
- - - - - moderately severe   45.2
- - - - - none   45.8
- - - - - profound   44.5
- - - - - severe   45.0
- - - - - unspecified   45.8
- - - - total hearing loss, other ear   44.1
- - moderate
- - - bilateral   45.4
- - - one ear
- - - - hearing impairment, other ear
- - - - - mild   45.5
- - - - - moderately severe   45.2
- - - - - none   45.6
- - - - - profound   44.4
- - - - - severe   45.0
- - - - - unspecified   45.6
- - - - total hearing loss, other ear   44.0
- - moderately severe
- - - better ear   43.3
- - - bilateral   43.2
- - - one ear
- - - - hearing impairment, other ear
- - - - - mild   45.2
- - - - - moderate   45.2
- - - - - none   45.3

Impairment - *continued*
- mechanical - *continued*
- - hip - *continued*
- - - one side - *continued*
- - - - ankle, foot or toe 71.95
- - - - knee or leg 71.94
- - internal organ NEC 60.3
- - knee 71.6-
- - - one side, with other side
- - - - ankle, foot or toe 71.96
- - - - hip or thigh 71.94
- - leg 71.6-
- - - one side, with other side
- - - - ankle, foot or toe 71.96
- - - - hip or thigh 71.94
- - limb NEC 71.99
- - - mixed type - *see* categories
      71.0-71.7 with 4th digit 8
- - lower limb NEC 71.93
- - - and upper limb 71.98
- - - both NEC 71.97
- - - due to unequal length of legs 71.92
- - metacarpus (and carpus) 71.3-
- - metatarsal joint 71.7-
- - neck NEC 70.41
- - shoulder 71.0-
- - subtaloid joint 71.7-
- - tarsal joint 71.7-
- - thigh 71.5-
- - - one side, with other side
- - - - ankle, foot or toe 71.95
- - - - knee or leg 71.94
- - thumb 71.4-
- - toe NEC 71.91
- - - bilateral 71.90
- - - one side, with other side
- - - - hip or thigh 71.95
- - - - knee or leg 71.96
- - upper
- - - arm, one side, with other side
- - - - finger 71.83
- - - - forearm 71.81
- - - - hand 71.82
- - - - wrist 71.82
- - - limb NEC 71.89
- - - - and lower limb 71.98
- - - - both NEC 71.88
- - - - more than one region 71.80
- - upper arm 71.0-
- - wrist 71.2-
- - - and hand 71.3-
- - - one side, with other side
- - - - finger 71.86
- - - - forearm 71.84
- - - - upper arm 71.82
- memory NEC (for) 16.9
- - figures 15.6

Impairment - *continued*
- memory NEC - *continued*
- - long-term events 15.1
- - past events 15.0
- - recent events 15.2
- - shapes 15.4
- - specified type NEC 16.8
- - words 15.5
- metabolic NEC 93.9
- - specified type NEC 93.8
- micturition NEC 63.7
- mood NEC 26.9
- - specified type NEC 26.88
- motivation 25.81
- motor NEC
- - and mechanical - *see* Impairment,
      mechanical and motor
- - head NEC 70.32
- - limb(s) NEC 74.9-
- - - four 74.6-
- - - lower NEC 74.4-
- - - - both 74.3-
- - - - with upper, same side 74.5-
- - - mixed type - *see* categories
      74.0-74.9 with 4th digit 8
- - - specified
- - - - combinations NEC 74.8-
- - - - type NEC - *see* categories
      74.0-74.9 with 4th digit 7
- - - three 74.6-
- - - upper NEC 74.2-
- - - - both 74.0-
- - - - dominant 74.1-
- - - - with lower, same side 74.5-
- - neck NEC 70.42
- - or analogous functional of internal
      organs 60.5
- - - combinations NEC 60.8
- multiple NEC 90.9
- - all classes 90.0
- - mental functions and speech 90.2
- - - and special senses (and viscera) (and
      skeleton) 90.1
- - special senses 90.4
- - - and viscera and skeleton 90.3
- - specified classes NEC 90.8
- - viscera and skeleton 90.5
- nasal function NEC 69.5
- neurological control of speech organs
      NEC 35.6
- night vision 57.6
- nipples NEC 67.2
- nonverbal "grammar" 36.0
- ocular NEC 58.9
- - ill-defined 58.7
- - motility NEC 57.4
- - specified type NEC 58.8

J

K

L

Lability, emotional 26.6
Lack of
− coordination NEC - *see* categories
  74.0-74.9 with 4th digit 5
− − complete - *see* categories 74.0-74.9
  with 4th digit 4
− humor 38.2
− initiative 27.0
− voluntary movement 28.1
Laryngeal palsy 35.6
Larynx
− artificial 35.0
− deficiency 35.1
Liability to falls 48.5
Libido decreased 25.3
Life support devices in use 94.0
Light sensitivity 57.8
Limping NEC 74.97
Lordosis 70.50
Loss (of)
− ability to distinguish fantasy from reality
  23.5
− appetite 25.0
− hearing
− − profound (bilateral) NEC 41.9
− − total NEC 41.9
− − − bilateral 41.0
− − − one ear NEC 44.9
− − − − hearing impairment, other ear
− − − − − mild 44.1
− − − − − moderate 44.0
− − − − − moderately severe 42.1
− − − − − none 44.2

Loss - *continued*
− hearing - *continued*
− − total NEC - *continued*
− − − one ear NEC - *continued*
− − − − hearing impairment, other
  ear - *continued*
− − − − − profound 41.1
− − − − − severe 42.0
− − − − − unspecified 44.3
− interests 27.1
− learned skills 14.3
− libido 25.3
− memory - *see* Amnesia
− menstrual, excessive 64.6
− movement, limb, NEC - *see* categories
  71.0-71.7 with 4th digit 7
− − bilateral - *see* categories 71.0-71.7
  with 4th digit 6
− − total NEC - *see* categories 71.0-71.7
  with 4th digit 1
− − − bilateral - *see* categories 71.0-71.7
  with 4th digit 0
− vision NEC (*see also* Impairment,
  vision) 55.9
− − transient 57.7
− voice production 35.2
− weight 93.5
Low vision NEC 53.9
− both eyes 53.8
− one eye with blindness, other eye 52.9
Lumbago 96.3
Lymphedema
− limb (lower) (upper) 86.5-

M

Macropsy experiences 23.4
Malformation congenital (limb) NEC 85.9-
− specified type NEC 85.8-
Malnutrition 93.4
Malocclusion 70.11
Malposition internal sex organ NEC 67.5
Mannerism
− facial NEC 70.22
− postural 70.55
Memory
− illusions 16.1
− impairment NEC (for) 16.8
− − figures 15.6
− − long-term events 15.1

Memory - *continued*
− impairment NEC - *continued*
− − past events 15.0
− − recent events 15.2
− − shapes 15.4
− − words 15.5
− − unspecified 16.9
Menorrhagia 64.6
Mental
− deficiency - *see* Mental, retardation
− retardation NEC 13.9
− − mild 13.0
− − moderate 12
− − profound 10

Mental - *continued*
- retardation NEC - *continued*
- - severe 11
- - specified type NEC 13.8
Microcephaly 81.1
Microspy experiences 23.4
Micturition, frequency 63.2
Mirror
- hand 85.6-
- writing 34.4
Misinterpretation 19.4
Mood
- impairment NEC 26.9
- - specified type NEC 26.88
- instability 26.6
- swings (frequent) 26.6
Moron 13.0
Movement
- abnormal, idiosyncratic, repetitive or
  stylized
- - facial 70.22
- - head 70.31

Movement - *continued*
- abnormal - *continued*
- - limb - *see* categories 74.0-74.9 with
  4th digit 3
- - - complete - *see* categories 74.0-74.9
  with 4th digit 2
- - postural 70.55
- involuntary
- - body 70.54
- - facial 70.21
- - limb - *see* categories 74.0-74.9 with
  4th digit 3
- - - complete - *see* categories 74.0-74.9
  with 4th digit 2
- masticatory 70.21
Mucus, rectal 62.8
Mumbling 35.5
Murmurs (cardiac) 61.2
Mutism 30.0
- akinetic 20.7
- deaf 40

N

Narcolepsy 22.3
Narrowing (of)
- attention span 24.2
- field of consciousness 20.2
Nasal obstruction 69.4
Nausea 62.0
Negativism 27.3

Nonsocial speech 37.6
Numbness (limb) NEC 98.6
- head 95.7
- lower limb 98.6
- trunk 96.7
- upper limb 97.7
Nystagmus 57.4

O

Obesity 70.64
Obsessional
- ideas 17.6
- traits 29.5
Obstruction
- esophageal 60.1
- gastric 60.1
- genital 66.5
- intestinal 60.2
- nasal 69.4
- outflow, urine 63.4
- tracheobronchial 60.0
- tubal 66.5
- urinary 63.4
Oligophrenia - *see* Mental, retardation

Orifice
- abnormal NEC 88.9
- - specified type NEC 88.8
- artificial NEC 88.7
Orthopnea 61.0
Otorrhea 49.2
Outbursts, angry 26.5
Outflow obstruction of micturation 63.4
Overactivity NEC 28.4
Overcompliance 27.2
Overflow incontinence 63.4
Overgrowth, limbs (lower) (upper) 85.4-
Overtalkativeness 28.4
Overvalued ideas 18.1

P

Pacemaker in situ 94.0
Pain (in)
– abdominal 62.3
– back 96.3
– chest NEC 61.4
– – on exercise 61.3
– ear 49.3
– eye 58.7
– facial 95.3
– generalized 94.2
– head NEC 95.4
– lower limb NEC 98.3
– – on exercise 61.5
– neck 96.3
– rectal 62.8
– trunk (region) NEC 96.4
– upper limb NEC 97.4
– – on exercise 97.3
Palpitation 61.6
Palsy - *see also* Paralysis
– diaphragmatic 60.4
– facial 70.20
– laryngeal 35.6
Panic attacks 26.01
Paralysis NEC
– facial 70.20
– limb(s) NEC 73.9-
– – flaccid (partial) NEC - *see* categories
  73.0-73.9 with 4th digit 5
– – – complete - *see* categories 73.0-73.9
  with 4th digit 4
– – – total NEC - *see* categories 73.0-73.9
  with 4th digit 3
– – – – complete - *see* categories
  73.0-73.9 with 4th digit 2
– – four 73.7-
– – lower NEC 73.4-
– – – and upper, same side 73.5-
– – – both 73.3-
– – spastic NEC 73.91
– – – complete 73.90
– – – four NEC 72.7
– – – – complete 72.6
– – – – lower NEC 73.41
– – – – – and upper, same side 72.2
– – – – – complete 72.1
– – – – – – with involvement of speech
  72.0
– – – – both 72.4
– – – – – complete 72.3
– – – – complete 73.40
– – – more than one NEC 72.9
– – – – specified combinations NEC
  72.8
– – – three 72.5

Paralysis NEC - *continued*
– limb(s) NEC - *continued*
– – spastic NEC - *continued*
– – – upper NEC 73.21
– – – – and lower, same side 72.2
– – – – – complete 72.1
– – – – – – with involvement of speech
  72.0
– – – – both NEC 73.01
– – – – – complete 73.00
– – – – complete 73.20
– – – – dominant NEC 73.11
– – – – – complete 73.10
– – specified combinations NEC 73.8-
– – three 73.6-
– – upper NEC 73.2-
– – – and lower, same side 73.5-
– – – both 73.0-
– – – dominant 73.1-
Paramnesia 16.1
Paraparesis (spastic) 72.4
Paraplegia (spastic) 72.3
Paresthesia - *see* Numbness
Pathological
– affect 20.3
– anxiety 26.00
– craving (alcohol) (drug) 25.7
Perception, false NEC 23.29
– specified type NEC 23.28
Peromelia - *see* Deficiency, transverse
Perplexity 29.81
Perseveration 17.4
Personality disorder 29.9
Petit mal (*see also* Epilepsy) 21.5
Phantom limb experiences 23.32
Phobias NEC 29.6
Phocomelia - *see* Deficiency, longitudinal
Pigmentation (skin)
– head 82.2
– limb (lower) (upper) 87.0-
– trunk 83.2
Piles 62.8
Pill (contraceptive) in use 64.0
Polydactylism 85.6-
Polydipsia 93.7
Polyuria 63.2
Postvasectomy 64.0
Poverty (of)
– speech content 38.5
– thought content 18.0
Pregnant 99.0
Prickling (lower limb) 98.8
– upper limb 97.8
Procidentia (uteri) 67.4
Prognathism 70.12

Q

R

S

Speech - *continued*
- non-social   37.6
- restricted   38.4
- slurred   35.5
Spells, blank   24.4
Spinal curvature   70.50
Splenunculus   66.3
Sputum   61.7
Stammering   37.0
State
- confusional   20.4
- dissociative   20.5
- hypnotic   20.6
- post-concussional   20.1
- trance-like   20.6
- twilight   20.3
Stature
- short   70.60
- unduly tall   70.61
Stereotypies
- facial   70.22
- postural   70.55
Sterility   64.1
Stiffness, limbs, NEC - *see* categories
    74.0-74.9 with 4th digit 1
- complete - *see* categories 74.0-74.9 with
    4th digit 0
- in mechanical impairment - *see* categories
    71.0-71.7 with 4th digit 7
- - bilateral - *see* categories 71.0-71.7
    with 4th digit 6

Strabismus   57.3
Strain
- eye   58.7
Stridor   61.1
Stupor   20.0
Stuttering   37.0
Subfertility   64.2
Substitute voice   35.0
Suspiciousness   29.0
Swelling
- limb (lower) (upper) NEC   86.6-
- - complete   86.5-
- part of head   82.1
- tissues
- - limb (lower) (upper)   86.4-
- trunk   83.1
Syncope   21.6
Syndactylia
- simple   84.4-
- skeletal   84.6-
- soft tissue   84.5-
Syndrome
- Apert   84.6-
- shoulder-hand   71.80
- transitional   20.1
Synonychia   84.5-
Synostosis   84.1-

T

Tachycardia   61.6
Tallness, undue   70.61
Temperature change (limb) NEC   98.2
- head   95.2
- lower limb   98.2
- trunk   96.2
- upper limb   97.2
Tetraparesis (spastic)   72.7
Tetraplegia (spastic)   72.6
Thinking - *see* condition
Thinness, undue   70.63
Thought - *see* condition
Throbbing, head   95.5
Tics   70.21
Tightness - *see also* Ache
- head   95.5
Time-standing-still   23.4
Tingling - *see* Numbness

Tinnitus   47.2
Titubation   70.31
Toothache   68.3
Torticollis   70.40
Tracheostomy   88.0
Traits
- histrionic   29.80
- obsessional   29.5
Trance-like state   20.6
Transplantation, renal   65.60
Transposition of viscera   66.2
Tremor NEC   74.92
- limb - *see* categories 74.0-74.9 with 4th
    digit 2
Trigger digit   84.2-
Trismus   70.10
Tumor
- head   82.1

Tumor - *continued*
- limb (lower) (upper) 86.4-
- trunk 83.1

Tunnel vision 56.6
Twilight state 20.3

U

Ugliness (marked) 82.8
Unconsciousness 20.0
Uncooperativeness 29.7
Underactivity NEC 28.1
Underdevelopment, lower jaw 70.13
Undescended testicle 67.5
Undue
- insensitivity to pain 92.5
- susceptibility (of) (to)
- - fracture NEC 92.2

Undue - *continued*
- susceptibility - *continued*
- - pressure sores 92.3
- - tissues NEC 92.6
- - trauma NEC 92.9
- - - specified type NEC 92.8
- tallness 70.61
- thinness 70.63
Urethritis 67.3

V

Vaginal
- bleeding 64.6
- discharge 67.3
Vaginitis 67.3
Varicose veins 87.3-
Vertigo 48.0
Violence 29.7
Vision loss NEC 55.9
- transient 57.7

Voice
- abnormally quiet 36.3
- breathy 36.6
- expressionless 36.1
- flat tone 36.1
- harsh 36.6
Vomiting 62.1
Vulnerability, excessive 29.2

W

Wasting
- head 82.0
- limb (lower) (upper) NEC 86.1-
- - complete 86.0-
- trunk 83.0
Weakness (generalized) NEC 94.5
- limbs - *see* categories 73.0-73.9 with 4th
  digit 6
Wears correcting lenses (giving
  (near-)normal vision) 57.0

Weight
- gain 93.6
- loss 93.5
Wetting - *see* Incontinence, urinary
Wheezing 61.1
Withdrawal, social 29.1
Worrying 29.4

X Y Z

SECTION 3

CLASSIFICATION OF DISABILITIES

List of two-digit categories
1 Behaviour disabilities
2 Communication disabilities
3 Personal care disabilities
4 Locomotor disabilities
5 Body disposition disabilities
6 Dexterity disabilities
7 Situational disabilities
8 Particular skill disabilities
9 Other activity restrictions
Supplementary gradings
Guidance on assignment

DISABILITY

Definition   In the context of health experience, a disability is any restriction or lack (resulting from an impairment) of ability to perform an activity in the manner or within the range considered normal for a human being

Characteristics   Disability is characterized by excesses or deficiencies of customarily expected activity performance and behaviour, and these may be temporary or permanent, reversible or irreversible, and progressive or regressive. Disabilities may arise as a direct consequence of impairment or as a response by the individual, particularly psychologically, to a physical, sensory, or other impairment. Disability represents objectification of an impairment, and as such it reflects disturbances at the level of the person

Disability is concerned with abilities, in the form of composite activities and behaviours, that are generally accepted as essential components of everyday life. Examples include disturbances in behaving in an appropriate manner, in personal care (such as excretory control and the ability to wash and feed oneself), in the performance of other activities of daily living, and in locomotor activities (such as the ability to walk)

LIST OF TWO-DIGIT CATEGORIES OF DISABILITY

1   **BEHAVIOUR DISABILITIES**

Awareness disabilities (10-16)

10	Self-awareness disability
11	Disability relating to location in time and space
12	Other identification disability
13	Personal safety disability
14	Disability relating to situational behaviour
15	Knowledge acquisition disability
16	Other educational disability

Disabilities in relations (17-19)

17	Family role disability
18	Occupational role disability
19	Other behaviour disability

2   **COMMUNICATION DISABILITIES**

Speaking disabilities (20-22)

20	Disability in understanding speech
21	Disability in talking
22	Other speaking disability

Listening disabilities (23-24)

23	Disability in listening to speech
24	Other listening disability

Seeing disabilities (25-27)

25	Disability in gross visual tasks
26	Disability in detailed visual tasks
27	Other disability in seeing and related activities

Other communication disabilities (28-29)

28   Disability in writing
29   Other communication disability

3   PERSONAL CARE DISABILITIES

Excretion disabilities (30-32)

30   Controlled excretory difficulty
31   Uncontrolled excretory difficulty
32   Other excretion disability

Personal hygiene disabilities (33-34)

33   Bathing disability
34   Other personal hygiene disability

Dressing disabilities (35-36)

35   Clothing disability
36   Other dressing disability

Feeding and other personal care disabilities (37-39)

37   Disability in preliminaries to feeding
38   Other feeding disability
39   Other personal çare disability

4   LOCOMOTOR DISABILITIES

Ambulation disabilities (40-45)

40   Walking disability
41   Traversing disability
42   Climbing stairs disability
43   Other climbing disability
44   Running disability
45   Other ambulation disability

Confining disabilities (46-47)

46   Transfer disability
47   Transport disability

Other locomotor disabilities (48-49)

48   Lifting disability
49   Other locomotor disability

5   BODY DISPOSITION DISABILITIES

Domestic disability (50-51)

50   Subsistence disability
51   Household disability

Body movement disabilities (52-27)

52   Retrieval disability
53   Reaching disability
54   Other disability in arm function
55   Kneeling disability
56   Crouching disability
57   Other body movement disability

Other body disposition disabilities (58-59)

58   Postural disability
59   Other body disposition disability

6   DEXTERITY DISABILITIES

Daily activity disabilities (60-61)

60   Environmental modulation disability
61   Other daily activity disability

Manual activity disabilities (62-66)

62   Fingering disability
63   Gripping disability
64   Holding disability
65   Handedness disability
66   Other manual activity disability

Other dexterity disabilities (67-69)

67   Foot control disability
68   Other body control disability
69   Other dexterity disability

7   SITUATIONAL DISABILITIES

Dependence and endurance disabilities (70-71)

70   Circumstantial dependence
71   Disability in endurance

Environmental disabilities (72-77)

72   Disability relating to temperature tolerance
73   Disability relating to tolerance of other climatic features
74   Disability relating to tolerance of noise
75   Disability relating to tolerance of illumination
76   Disability relating to tolerance of work stresses
77   Disability relating to tolerance of other environmental factors

Other situational disabilities (78)

78   Other situational disability

8   PARTICULAR SKILL DISABILITIES

9   OTHER ACTIVITY RESTRICTIONS

1 BEHAVIOUR DISABILITIES

Refer to an individual's awareness and ability to conduct himself, both in
everyday activities and towards others, and including the ability to learn

Excludes : communication disabilities (2)

AWARENESS DISABILITIES (10 - 16)
Awareness refers to having knowledge

10 Self-awareness disability

Includes : disturbance of the ability to develop or maintain a
mental representation of the identity of the individual's
self or body ("body image") and its continuity over
time; and disturbance of behaviour resulting from interference with consciousness or sense of identity and confusion (inappropriate interpretation of and response to
external events, which expresses itself in agitation, restlessness, and noisiness)

10.0 *Transient self-awareness disability*

10.1 *Disability in body image orientation*

Includes : disturbance in the mental representation of the individual's body, such as inability in right-left differentiation, "phantom limb" experiences, and other related
phenomena

10.2 *Personal uncleanliness*

Includes : neglect of shaving or state of hair, and dirty clothing

10.3 *Other disturbance of appearance*

Includes : careless dress or make-up, and appearance that is
bizarre (such as "secret documents" and special clothes
or ornaments with idiosyncratic meaning, which may
be related to delusions), of very inappropriate taste,
or conspicuously out of fashion

10.4 *Other disturbance of self-presentation*

Includes : disturbance of the ability to present a favourable image
in social situations, such as by inattention to supportive
social routines (e.g., greetings, partings, giving thanks,
apologizing, excusing, and reciprocation of these), and
lack of "presence" (e.g., total absence of originality, or
excessive conformity in demeanour)

Excludes : intended unconventional behaviour (which is not a disability)

10.8   *Other*

10.9   *Unspecified*

11   Disability relating to location in time and space

Includes :   disturbance of the ability of the individual to correctly locate external objects, events, and himself in relation to the dimensions of time and space

11.0   *Transient disability relating to location in time and space*

11.8   *Other*

11.9   *Unspecified*

12   Other identification disability

Includes :   disturbance of the ability to identify objects and persons correctly

12.0   *Transient disability in identifying objects and persons*

12.1   *Conduct out of context*

Conduct that is generally appropriate but which is inappropriate to the place, time, or stage of maturation

Includes :   cultural shock (such as in immigrants), moving in different identities (e.g., transvestism and passing, such as black passing for white), pseudo-feeble-mindedness, and breaking taboos

12.8   *Other*

12.9   *Unspecified*

13   Personal safety disability

Includes :   disturbance of the ability to avoid hazards to the integrity of the individual's body, such as being in hazard from self-injury or from inability to safeguard self from danger

13.0   *Liability to self-injury*

Includes :   risk of suicide or self-inflicted injury

13.1   *Personal safety disability in special situations*

Includes :   being in hazard in special situations, such as those related to travel and transport, occupation, and recreation, including sport

Excludes :   occupational role disability (18)

13.2   *Conduct potentially dangerous to the individual himself*

Includes :   leaving gas taps or fires on

13.3   *Other irresponsible conduct*
        Includes :   tossing lighted matches on carpet
13.4   *Getting lost*
13.5   *Other wandering*
        Includes :   when inappropriately clad
13.8   *Other*
13.9   *Unspecified*

14   Disability relating to situational behaviour
        Includes :   disturbance of the capacity to register and understand
                     relations between objects and persons in situations of
                     daily living
        Excludes :   personal safety disability in special situations (13.1)
14.0   *Situation comprehension disability*
        Includes :   disturbance of the capacity to perceive, register, or
                     understand relations between things and people
14.1   *Situation interpretation disability*
        Includes :   false interpretation of the relations between and mean-
                     ing of things and people
14.2   *Situation coping disability*
        Includes :   disturbance of the ability to perform everyday activi-
                     ties in specific situations, such as outside the home or
                     in the presence of particular animals or other objects
        Excludes :   disability in crisis conduct (18.6)
14.8   *Other*
14.9   *Unspecified*

15   Knowledge acquisition disability
        Includes :   general disturbance of the ability to learn, such as may
                     arise from impairments of intellect or of the ability to
                     learn new skills

16   Other educational disability
        Includes :   other inability to benefit from educational opportunities
                     because of disturbance of specific individual capacities
                     for acquiring, processing, and retaining new information
        Excludes :   those arising from communication (2) and other dis-
                     abilities (3 - 7)

16.9   *Unspecified*

Includes :   slowing of mental functions NOS

DISABILITIES IN RELATIONS (17 - 19)

17   **Family role disability**

17.0   *Disability in participation in household activities*

Includes :   customary common activities such as having meals together, doing domestic chores, going out or visiting together, playing games, and watching television, and conduct during these activities, as well as household decision-making, such as decisions about children and money

17.1   *Disability in affective partnership role*

Includes :   affective relationship with steady partner or spouse, and communication (such as talking about children, news, and ordinary events), ability to show affection and warmth (but excluding culturally customary outbursts of anger or irritability), and engendering a feeling of being a source of support in the partner

17.2   *Other disability in affective partnership role*

Includes :   disturbance of sexual relations with steady partner (including occurrence of sexual intercourse and whether both individual and partner find sexual relations satisfactory)

17.3   *Parental role disability*

Includes :   undertaking and performance of child care tasks appropriate to the individual's position in household (such as feeding, putting to bed, or taking to school, for small children, and looking after child's needs, for older children) and taking interest in child (such as playing with, reading to, and taking interest in child's problems or school work)

17.8   *Other family role disability*

17.9   *Unspecified*

18   **Occupational role disability**

Includes :   disturbance of the ability to organize and participate in
routine activities connected with the occupation of time,
not just confined to the performance of work

Excludes :   situational disabilities (70 - 79)

18.0   *Disability in motivation*

Includes :   interference with the ability to work by virtue of
severe impairment of drive

18.1   *Disability in cooperation*

Includes :   inability to cooperate with others and to "give and take"
in social interaction

18.2   *Disability in work routine*

Includes :   other aspects of conformity to work routine (such as
going to work regularly and on time, and observing the
rules)

18.3   *Disability in organizing daily routine*

Includes :   disturbance of the ability to organize activities in temporal sequences, and difficulty in making decisions about
day-to-day matters

18.4   *Other disability in work performance*

Includes :   other inadequacy in performance and output

18.5   *Recreation disability*

Includes :   lack of interest in leisure activities (such as watching
television, listening to radio, reading newspapers or
books, participating in games, and hobbies) and in local
and world events (including efforts to obtain information)

18.6   *Disability in crisis conduct*

Includes :   unsatisfactory or inappropriate responses to incidents
(such as sickness, accident, or other incident affecting
family member or involving other people), emergencies
(such as fire), and other experiences customarily requiring quick decision and action

18.8   *Other occupational role disability*

Includes :   for individuals not working, their interest in obtaining
or returning to work and actual steps undertaken to
this end

Excludes :   other social role disability (19.2)

18.9 *Unspecified*

19 Other behaviour disability

Includes : disturbance of interpersonal relationships outside the household

Excludes : occupational role disability (18)

19.0 *Antisocial behaviour*

Includes : severely maladjusted, psychopathic, and delinquent

19.1 *Indifference to accepted social standards*

Includes : conduct that is embarrassing (such as making sexual suggestions or advances, or lacking restraint in scratching genitals or in passing loud flatus), irreverent (such as singing, making facetious silly jokes or flippant remarks, or being unduly familiar), or histrionic (such as expression of feelings in an exaggerated, dramatic, or histrionic manner)

19.2 *Other social role disability*

Includes : overt conduct by the individual involving arguments, arrogance, anger, marked irritability, or other friction arising in social situations outside own home (such as with supervisors, co-workers, or customers, if the individual engages in outside work; with neighbours and other people in the community, if the individual has a domestic role; with teachers, administrators, and fellow students, if the individual is a student; and with fellow inhabitants, if the individual lives in communal accommodation)

Excludes : self-awareness (10) and identification disabilities (11 - 12)

19.3 *Other personality disability*

Includes : other excess or lack of any customary trait of personality NOS

19.4 *Other severe behaviour disorder*

Includes : other disturbance of behaviour (such as aggressiveness, destructiveness, extreme overactivity, and attention-seeking) that presents problems in management and that are NEC

19.8 *Other*

19.9 *Unspecified*

Includes : behaviour disorder NOS

2   COMMUNICATION DISABILITIES

Refer to an individual's ability to generate and emit messages, and to receive and understand messages

SPEAKING DISABILITIES (20 - 22)

20   Disability in understanding speech
    Includes :   loss or restriction of the ability to understand the meaning of verbal messages
    Excludes :   listening disabilities (23) and situation-related difficulties such as lack of knowledge of a local language

21   Disability in talking
    Includes :   loss or restriction of the ability to produce audible verbal messages and to convey meaning through speech

22   Other speaking disability
22.0   *Disability in understanding other audible messages*
    Excludes :   listening disabilities (24)
22.1   *Disability in expression through substitute language codes*
    Includes :   loss or restriction of the ability to convey information by a code of sign language
22.2   *Other disability with substitute language codes*
    Includes :   loss or reduction of the ability to receive information by a code of sign language
22.8   *Other*
22.9   *Unspecified*

LISTENING DISABILITIES (23 - 24)

23   Disability in listening to speech
    Includes :   loss or reduction of the ability to receive verbal messages

24   Other listening disability
    Includes :   loss or reduction of the ability to receive other audible messages

SEEING DISABILITIES (25 - 27)

25   Disability in gross visual tasks

Includes :   loss or reduction of the ability to execute tasks requiring adequate distant or peripheral vision

26   Disability in detailed visual tasks

Includes :   loss or reduction of the ability to execute tasks requiring adequate visual acuity, such as reading, recognition of faces, writing, and visual manipulation

27   Other disability in seeing and related activities

Excludes :   disability related to tolerance of illumination (75)

27.0   *Disability in night vision*

27.1   *Disability in colour recognition*

27.2   *Disability in comprehending written messages*

Includes :   loss or reduction of the ability to decode and understand written messages

27.3   *Other disability in reading written language*

Includes :   difficulty with speed or endurance

27.4   *Disability in reading other systems of notation*

Includes :   loss or reduction of the ability to read Braille by an individual disabled in near sight who had previously had this ability, or difficulty in learning this system of notation by an individual disabled in near sight

27.5   *Disability in lip reading*

Includes :   loss or reduction of the ability to lip-read by an individual disabled in listening who had previously had this ability, or difficulty in learning this skill by an individual disabled in listening

27.8   *Other*

27.9   *Unspecified*

OTHER COMMUNICATION DISABILITIES (28 - 29)

28   Disability in writing

Includes :   loss or reduction of the ability to encode language into written words and to execute written messages or to make marks

29   Other communication disability

29.0   *Disability in symbolic communication*

Includes :   loss or restriction of the ability to understand signs and symbols associated with conventional codes (e.g., traffic lights and signs, and pictograms) and to read maps, simple diagrams, and other schematic representations of objects

29.1   *Other disability in nonverbal expression*

Includes :   loss or restriction of the ability to convey information by gesture, expression, and related means

29.2   *Other disability in nonverbal communication*

Includes :   loss or restriction of the ability to receive information by gesture, expression, and related means

29.8   *Other*

29.9   *Unspecified*

Includes :   communication disability NOS

3   PERSONAL CARE DISABILITIES

Refer to an individual's ability to look after himself in regard to basic physiological activities, such as excretion and feeding, and to caring for himself, such as with hygiene and dressing

EXCRETION DISABILITIES (30-32)

30   **Controlled excretory difficulty**
Control relates to mitigation of the consequences of excretory difficulty by effecting a degree of regulation, either by adaptive devices, electrical stimulators, special protective clothing, or by some other means, so that an effectively customary existence becomes possible

30.0   *Control by adaptive devices*

30.1   *Control by electrical stimulators*

30.2   *Gastrointestinal diversion*
Includes : ileostomy and colostomy
Excludes : internal short-circuit operations (70.5)

30.3   *Indwelling urinary catheter*

30.4   *Other urinary diversion*
Includes : with abnormal orifice (such as cystostomy)
Excludes : internal short-circuit operations (70.5)

30.5   *Control by special protective clothing*

30.8   *Other control of excretory difficulty*

30.9   *Unspecified*

31   **Uncontrolled excretory difficulty**

31.0   *Severe double incontinence*
Frequency every night and every day
Includes :   soiling (faecal incontinence) and wetting (incontinence of urine)

31.1   *Moderate double incontinence*
Frequency greater than once every week by night and by day

31.2   *Other double incontinence*

31.3   *Other faecal incontinence*

31.4   *Other urinary incontinence*

31.8   *Other uncontrolled incontinence*

31.9   *Unspecified*

32   **Other excretion disability**

32.0 *Associated with transfer difficulty at home*
Difficulty for the individual in transferring self to and from a lavatory at home

32.1 *Associated with transfer difficulty elsewhere*

32.2 *Other difficulty in using sanitary facilities*

32.8 *Other excretion disability*

32.9 *Unspecified*

PERSONAL HYGIENE DISABILITIES (33-34)

33　Bathing disability
Includes : having an all-over wash, washing the body and the back, and drying self thereafter

33.0 *Associated with transfer difficulty*
Difficulty for the individual in transferring self to and from a bath

33.1 *Other difficulty in using a bath*

33.2 *Difficulty in using a shower*

33.8 *Other bathing disability*

33.9 *Unspecified*

34　Other personal hygiene disability

34.0 *Washing face*

34.1 *Washing hair*
Includes : washing neck and ears

34.2 *Care of hands*
Includes : washing, and care of fingernails

34.3 *Care of feet*
Includes : washing, and care of toenails

34.4 *Post-excretion hygiene*

34.5 *Menstrual hygiene*

34.6 *Dental hygiene*

34.7 *Gender-specific care*
Includes : brushing and combing hair, and shaving

34.8 *Other*

34.9 *Unspecified*

DRESSING DISABILITIES (35-36)

35   **Clothing disability**
Excludes : footwear (36.1)

35.0   *Underclothes*

35.1   *Lower part of body*
Includes : putting on skirts and trousers

35.2   *Over arms and shoulders*
Includes : putting on jackets

35.3   *Over the head*
Includes : putting on blouses, shirts, and nightdresses

35.4   *Outer clothing*
Includes : putting on overalls, smocks, and overcoats

35.5   *Fastenings*
Includes : doing up buttons, hooks, and zips

35.8   *Other*

35.9   *Unspecified*

36   **Other dressing disability**

36.0   *Hosiery*
Includes : putting on socks and stockings

36.1   *Footwear*
Includes : putting on shoes and tying shoelaces

36.2   *Protective covering of hands*

36.3   *Headwear*

36.4   *Cosmetics*

36.5   *Other aspects of adornment*

36.8   *Other*

36.9   *Unspecified*

FEEDING AND OTHER PERSONAL CARE DISABILITIES (37-39)

37   **Disability in preliminaries to feeding**

37.0   *Dispensing beverages*
Includes : pouring tea

37.1	*Holding drinking vessel*	
37.2	*Dispensing food*	
	Includes : serving food	
37.3	*Making food ready*	
	Includes : cutting meat and buttering bread	
37.4	*Eating utensils*	
	Includes : holding cutlery and other eating utensils	
37.8	*Other*	
37.9	*Unspecified*	

38   Other feeding disability

37.1 *Holding drinking vessel*

37.2 *Dispensing food*
Includes : serving food

37.3 *Making food ready*
Includes : cutting meat and buttering bread

37.4 *Eating utensils*
Includes : holding cutlery and other eating utensils

37.8 *Other*

37.9 *Unspecified*

38   Other feeding disability

38.0 *Drinking*
Includes : conveying beverages to mouth and consuming (such as sipping)

38.1 *Eating*
Includes : conveying food to mouth and ingesting

38.2 *Chewing*
Includes : mastication

38.3 *Swallowing*

38.4 *Gastrostomy*

38.5 *Poor appetite*

38.8 *Other*

38.9 *Unspecified*

39   Other personal care disability

39.0 *Difficulty in getting to bed*
Includes : difficulty in getting up, and inability to make the decision to go to bed
Excludes : transfer disability (46)

39.1 *Difficulty in bed*
Includes : difficulty in managing bedclothes

39.8 *Other*

39.9 *Unspecified*

4 LOCOMOTOR DISABILITIES

Refer to an individual's ability to execute distinctive activities associated with moving, both himself and objects, from place to place

Excludes : overall mobility and consideration of the degree to which this may be restored by aids (code under the handicap classification), and also disabilities arising from diminished endurance (71)

AMBULATION DISABILITIES (40-45)

40 **Walking disability**
Includes : ambulation on flat terrain
Excludes : negotiation of discontinuities in terrain (41-43)

41 **Traversing disability**
Includes : negotiation of discontinuities in terrain such as the occasional step between different levels
Excludes : flights of stairs (42) and other aspects of climbing (43)

42 **Climbing stairs disability**
Includes : negotiation of flights of stairs and similar man-made obstacles such as ladders
Excludes : the occasional step (41)

43 **Other climbing disability**
Includes : natural obstacles

44 **Running disability**

45 **Other ambulation disability**

CONFINING DISABILITIES (46-47)

46 **Transfer disability**
Excludes : those related to excretion (32), bathing (33), and transport (47)

46.0 *Transfer from lying*
Includes : difficulty in rising from and lying down on bed
Excludes : difficulties in getting to bed and getting up that are not related to the actual transfer (39.0)

46.1 *Transfer from sitting*
Includes : difficulty in getting in and out of chairs
Excludes : difficulty associated with getting on or off a lavatory (32) or in and out of a car (47.0)

46.2 *Standing transfer*
Includes : difficulty in standing transfer to or from bed associated with manipulative problems

46.3 *Reaching bed or chair*
Includes : difficulty in reaching a bed or chair

46.8 *Other*

46.9 *Unspecified*

47 Transport disability

47.0 *Personal transport*
Includes : difficulty such as transfer in and out of car or in using other forms of personal transport

47.1 *Other vehicles*
Includes : mounting and dismounting from public transport

47.2 *Other difficulty with remote shopping*
Includes : inaccessibility from location to which transported (such as that vehicles cannot be parked sufficiently close)
Excludes : neighbourhood shopping (50.0) and lack of availability of transport (which is a handicap)

47.7 *Other transport disability*

47.8 *Other confining disability*

47.9 *Unspecified*

OTHER LOCOMOTOR DISABILITIES (48-49)

48 Lifting disability
Includes : carrying
Excludes : difficulty in lifting and carrying related only to sustenance disability (50)

49 Other locomotor disability
Excludes : body movement disabilities (52-57)

5   BODY DISPOSITION DISABILITIES

Refer to an individual's ability to execute distinctive activities associated with the disposition of the parts of the body, and including derivative activities such as execution of tasks associated with the individual's domicile

> Excludes :   dexterity disabilities (6)

DOMESTIC DISABILITIES (50-51)

50   Subsistence disability

50.0   *Procuring sustenance*
Includes :   shopping in immediate neighbourhood
Excludes :   remote shopping associated with transport disability (47)

50.1   *Transporting sustenance*
Includes :   laying in supplies by transporting to home (such as carrying shopping)

50.2   *Opening containers*
Includes :   opening cans

50.3   *Preparing food*
Includes :   cutting and chopping

50.4   *Mixing food*
Includes :   beating

50.5   *Cooking solids*
Includes :   lifting and serving from pots and pans

50.6   *Cooking liquids*
Includes :   managing and pouring from containers of hot fluids

50.7   *Serving food*
Includes :   carrying trays

50.8   *Catering hygiene*
Includes :   washing up utensils after meals

50.9   *Other and unspecified*

51   Household disability

51.0   *Care of bedding*

51.1   *"Smalls" laundry*
Includes :   gentle hand washing (such as of small or delicate garments)

51.2   *Bulk laundry*
Includes :   washing large garments and household linen

51.3   *Drying laundry*
Includes :   wringing, hanging out, and spreading out

51.4   *Manual cleaning*
Includes :   wiping, dusting, rubbing, and polishing

51.5   *Assisted cleaning*
Includes :   sweeping and use of floor cleaner (such as vacuum cleaner)

51.6   *Care of dependants*
Includes :   helping children or other dependants with tasks such as feeding and dressing

51.8   *Other*
Excludes :   moving objects (61.3) and reaching or stretching up (53)

51.9   *Unspecified*

BODY MOVEMENT DISABILITIES (52 - 57)
Excludes :   those classifiable as domestic disabilities (50-51)

52   Retrieval disability
Includes :   picking up objects from floor, and bending
Excludes :   picking up and carrying small objects (61.3)

53   Reaching disability
Includes :   reaching or stretching up for objects

54   Other disability in arm function
Includes :   the ability to push or pull with the upper limbs

55   Kneeling disability

56   Crouching disability
Includes :   stooping

57   Other body movement disability

OTHER BODY DISPOSITION DISABILITIES (58-59)

58   Postural disability
Includes :   difficulty in attaining or maintaining postures (such as disturbance of balance)
Excludes :   those related to limited endurance (71)

59   Other body disposition disability

Includes : other difficulty in maintaining appropriate relations
           between different parts of the body

6   DEXTERITY DISABILITIES

Refer to adroitness and skill in bodily movements, including manipulative skills and the ability to regulate control mechanisms

Excludes :   ability to write or make marks (28)

DAILY ACTIVITY DISABILITIES (60-61)

60   Environmental modulation disability

60.0   *Security disability*
Includes :   operation of latches and other closures (such as door handles), and use of keys

60.1   *Ingress disability*
Includes :   opening and closing of doors

60.2   *Fire*
Includes :   kindling fire and striking matches

60.3   *Domestic appliances*
Includes :   use of taps, pumps, switches, and plugs

60.4   *Ventilation*
Includes :   opening windows

60.8   *Other*

60.9   *Unspecified*

61   Other daily activity disability

61.0   *Use of standard (dial) telephone*

61.1   *Currency*
Includes :   handling money

61.2   *Other fine movements*
Includes :   winding watches and clocks

61.3   *Moving objects*
Includes :   picking up and carrying small objects and avoiding dropping objects
Excludes :   retrieving objects (52)

61.4   *Handling objects*
Includes :   managing a newspaper

61.8   *Other*

61.9   *Unspecified*

MANUAL ACTIVITY DISABILITIES (62-66)
Excludes : writing disability (28)

62   **Fingering disability**
Includes : ability to manipulate with fingers

63   **Gripping disability**
Includes : ability to grasp or grip objects and move them

64   **Holding disability**
Includes : ability to immobilize objects by holding them

65   **Handedness disability**
Includes : disabled by virtue of being a sinistral in a predominantly
dextral culture

66   **Other manual activity disability**
Includes : other difficulty in coordination

OTHER DEXTERITY DISABILITIES (67-69)

67   **Foot control disability**
Includes : ability to use foot control mechanisms

68   **Other body control disability**
Includes : ability to use other parts of body to regulate control
mechanisms

69   **Other dexterity disability**

7   SITUATIONAL DISABILITIES

Although some of the difficulties incorporated in this section are not strictly disturbances of activity performance (in fact, some could more properly be conceived of as impairments), they have been included here for practical reasons — particularly in regard to reciprocal specification of the environment (see earlier section on the *Consequences of disease*)

DEPENDENCE AND ENDURANCE DISABILITIES (70-71)

70   **Circumstantial dependence**
Includes : dependence for continued existence and activity upon life-sustaining equipment or special procedures or care

70.1   *Dependent on external mechanical equipment*
Includes : dependence on any form of external life-saving machine, such as an aspirator, a respirator, and a kidney (dialysis) machine, or any form of electromechanical device for the sustenance or extension of activity potential, such as Possum and related enabling devices

70.2   *Dependent on internal devices for life sustenance*
Includes : cardiac pacemaker

70.3   *Dependent on other internal devices*
Includes : cardiac valve prostheses and joint replacements

70.4   *Dependent on organ transplantation*
Includes : post-transplantation status

70.5   *Dependent on other alterations to the internal environment of the body*
Includes : internal short-circuit operations and existence of artificial orifices
Excludes : organ removal without functional consequences (such as appendicectomy or cholecystectomy), and artificial orifices related to excretion (30) or feeding (38)

70.6   *Dependent on special diet*
Includes : inability to partake of the meals customary to the individual's culture

70.8   *Dependent on other forms of special care*
Excludes : dependence on the help of another individual (see *Supplementary gradings of disability*)

70.9   *Unspecified dependence*

71   **Disability in endurance**

71.0   *Disability in sustaining positions*
          Includes : sitting and standing

71.1   *Disability in exercise tolerance*

71.2   *Disability in other aspects of physical endurance*

71.8   *Other disability in endurance*

71.9   *Unspecified*

ENVIRONMENTAL DISABILITIES (72-77)

72   **Disability relating to temperature tolerance**

72.0   *Tolerance of cold*

72.1   *Tolerance of heat*

72.8   *Tolerance of other aspect of ventilation*

72.9   *Unspecified*

73   **Disability relating to tolerance of other climatic features**

73.0   *Tolerance of ultraviolet light*
          Includes : sunlight
          Excludes : intolerance of bright illumination (75.0)

73.1   *Tolerance of humidity*

73.2   *Tolerance of extremes of barometric pressure*
          Includes : intolerance of pressurization associated with flying

73.9   *Unspecified*

74   **Disability relating to tolerance of noise**

75   **Disability relating to tolerance of illumination**

75.0   *Tolerance of bright illumination*

75.1   *Tolerance of fluctuation in illumination*

75.8   *Other*

75.9   *Unspecified*

76   Disability relating to tolerance of work stresses

Includes : inability to cope with the speed or other aspects of the pressure of work

Excludes : that attributable to occupational role disability (18)

77   Disability relating to tolerance of other environmental factors

77.0 *Tolerance of dust*

77.1 *Tolerance of other allergens*

77.2 *Undue susceptibility to chemical agents*
Includes : that associated with liver disease, and that arising from previous exposure to safe limits of toxic chemicals

77.3 *Undue susceptibility to other toxins*

77.4 *Undue susceptibility to ionizing radiation*
Includes : that arising from previous exposure to safe limits of irradiation

77.8 *Tolerance of other environmental factors*

77.9 *Unspecified*

OTHER SITUATIONAL DISABILITIES (78)

78   Other situational disability

Includes : generalized activity restrictions arising from such reasons as the individual's being delicate or unduly susceptible to trauma

8   PARTICULAR SKILL DISABILITIES

Vocational resettlement calls for assessment of many aspects of the individual's abilities and accomplishments. These include :

i)   behavioural abilities, such as intelligence, drive, motivation (including attitude to rehabilitation), perception, awareness (including ability to see possibilities and limitations), learning ability (including openness to new ideas and learning potential), orientation for shape and space, concentration (including intensity and ability to be sustained), memory (for words, figures, and shapes, and long-term), and thinking (abstract and logical), as well as reaction to criticism, ability to cooperate, and other aspects of social relationships

ii)   task fulfilment abilities, such as capacity to plan tasks, problem solving (flexibility and resourcefulness), adaptability, independence in fulfilment, task motivation and interest, capacity to control own work and compare it with that of others, sensorimotor coordination, dexterity (fine and gross), accuracy, tidiness, punctuality, safety behaviour, endurance (both as regards sustaining full-time occupation and in relation to work circumstances, such as fatigue resistance), performance rate (both for repetitive and for complex tasks), and performance quality

Most of these attributes have already been accommodated, as appropriate, in the impairment and disability classifications. However, there is also a need to accommodate particular occupation-related physical and other skills that have not been included elsewhere. This need may vary in different contexts at present, and there is insufficient basis at the moment for development of a subclassification of such skills that might have universal application. Nevertheless this section has been provided in anticipation of these needs, in the hope that preliminary experience in the use of these classifications will indicate the most useful approach. It is hoped that individual users of the disability classification will develop their own tentative subclassifications for this section

9   OTHER ACTIVITY RESTRICTIONS

This section also has been made available so as to provide a means of meeting needs not satisfied in other parts of the classification. Again, it is hoped that individual users of the disability classification will develop their own tentative subclassifications for this section, so as to provide the basis for a more standardized scheme in the future

SUPPLEMENTARY GRADINGS OF DISABILITY

Severity   Most people concerned with helping individuals who have a disability usually qualify their assessments with a grading of the severity of restriction in activity performance. Provision has therefore been made for a fourth-digit supplement to disability classification assignments for this purpose

Outlook   Some users have expressed a wish to be able to codify the outlook for individuals who have a disability. Provision has therefore been made for an optional fifth-digit supplement to disability classification assignments for this purpose

Coding conventions   The structure of the disability classification is such that it may extend to a three-digit field. In order to avoid ambiguity, therefore, it is recommended that these supplementary gradings always be coded to the fourth and fifth digit positions, even if the classification is only being used at one or two digit levels

INTERVENTION AND SEVERITY

In everyday life, performance is very rarely an all-or-none characteristic, and most people acknowledge this fact by grading the severity of restriction. It is recommended that grading to the scale categories shown in the next section be recorded as a fourth-digit supplement to disability classification assignments; there are very few disabilities to which the standard scale categories are not applicable

As far as scale categories are concerned, there are four goals for intervention in regard to disability :

(i)   *Disability prevention,* when the individual is able to perform activities unaided and on his own without difficulty

(ii)   *Enhancement,* when the individual is able to perform activities unaided and on his own but only with difficulty

(iii)   *Supplementation,* when the individual is able to perform activities only with aid, including that of others

(iv)   *Substitution,* when the individual cannot perform activities, even with aid

These goals can be illustrated by different levels of disability in seeing. Thus :

Level (i)   the individual can carry out all visual tasks

Level (ii)   the individual's vision needs enhancement in order for him to
                  be able to carry out detailed visual tasks without difficulty;
                  enhancement may be accomplished directly, such as by the
                  use of reading glasses, or indirectly by adaptation, either by
                  adjustment of illumination or by complementary assistance
                  such as the use of large print

Level (iii)   the individual can accomplish gross visual tasks only by
                  supplementing his performance with aid; supplementation
                  may be *direct*, e.g., by the continuous use of appliances such
                  as powerful correcting lenses or by help from a guide dog, or,
                  with other types of physical disability, by the assistance of
                  other people, or *indirect*, e.g., by adjustment or adaptation
                  of the environment (for instance, by use of raised marks on
                  control gear, such as knobs, to allow tactile reinforcement of
                  precision in adjustment)

Level (iv)   the individual has no useful vision and so is dependent on
                  substitution to accomplish tasks that are customarily mediated
                  by vision; substitution may be accomplished in various ways,
                  such as by radio as a replacement for newspapers as a source
                  of news, by provision of talking books, or by provision of a
                  suitably adapted environment to eliminate hazards that the
                  individual usually avoids by reliance on his vision

At first it might be thought that these four levels could provide the basis for
a simple scaling of severity of disability. Certainly the categories have the
merit of being fairly easy to define, and hence to ascertain, and such a four-
point scale has been used quite widely. However, the categories are too broad
to indicate with enough precision the quality of intervention required to improve performance. Moreover, they are unequal in their scope; thus levels
i, ii, and iii can all refer to individuals who, under most circumstances, could
be regarded as being independent, whereas both levels iii and iv are susceptible
to subdivision that displays more sensitively the types of intervention required

SEVERITY OF DISABILITY
(optional fourth-digit supplement)

Definition
Severity of disability reflects the degree to which an individual's activity performance is restricted

Characteristics

Scale construct : the potential for intervention at the level of the individual to improve functional performance in relation to current status

Includes : indications of the potential to meet some unfulfilled needs in regard to disability

Excludes : severity of underlying impairments, and also the potential to reduce the individual's handicap (disadvantage) status, particularly by social policy and social welfare measures

Severity scale categories

0   *Not disabled* (not in categories 1 - 9)

Includes : no disability present (i.e., the individual can perform the activity or sustain the behaviour unaided and on his own without difficulty)

1   *Difficulty in performance* (not in categories 2 - 9)

Includes : difficulty present (i.e., the individual can perform the activity or sustain the behaviour unaided and on his own but only with difficulty)

2   *Aided performance* (not in categories 3 - 9)

Includes : aids and appliances necessary (i.e., the individual can perform the activity only with a physical aid or appliance)

Excludes : assistance by other people (category 3)

3   *Assisted performance* (not in categories 4 - 9)

Includes : the need for a helping hand (i.e., the individual can perform the activity or sustain the behaviour, whether augmented by aids or not, only with some assistance from another person)

4   *Dependent performance* (not in categories 5 - 9)

Includes : complete dependence on the presence of another person (i.e., the individual can perform the activity or sustain the behaviour, but only when someone is with him most of the time)

Excludes : inability (categories 5 and 6)

5   *Augmented inability* (not in categories 6 - 9)

         Includes :   activity impossible to achieve other than with the help of
                      another person, the latter needing an aid or appliance to
                      enable him to provide this help (for example, the individual
                      cannot be got out of bed other than by the use of a hoist);
                      behaviour can be sustained only in the presence of another
                      person and in a protected environment

6   *Complete inability* (not in categories 8 or 9)

         Includes :   activity or behaviour impossible to achieve or sustain (for
                      example, an individual who is bed-bound is also unable to
                      transfer)

8   *Not applicable*

         Includes :   severity grading not applicable to particular disability

9   *Severity unspecified*

It can be seen that the scale categories correspond to intervention goals in the
following manner :

Enhancement   scale category 1

Supplementation   scale categories 2 - 4

Substitution   scale categories 5 and 6

Rules for assignment

i   categorize an individual according to his activity performance, taking
         account of aids, appliances, and assistance needed to permit this level
         of accomplishment;

ii   aids and appliances that it is intended to provide or prescribe should
         not be taken into account — this would then permit use of the scale as
         a rough measure of what had been accomplished when such aid or
         appliance was provided;

iii   if doubt is experienced about the category to which a disability should
         be assigned, rate it to the less favourable category (i.e., that with a
         higher number)

ASSESSMENT OF OUTLOOK
(optional fifth-digit supplement)

Definition

Outlook reflects the likely course of the individual's disability status

Characteristics

Scale construct :   the potential for intervention at the level of the individual
                    to improve functional performance in relation to expected
                    future status

Includes :   indications of the potential to anticipate some needs in
                    regard to disability

Excludes :   prognosis for underlying impairments, other than to the
                    extent that disability status may correlate closely with the
                    outlook for the impairment
                    the potential to reduce the individual's handicap (disad-
                    vantage) status, particularly by social policy and social
                    welfare measures

Outlook scale categories

0   *Not disabled* (not in categories 1 - 9)

    Includes :   no disability present

1   *Recovery potential* (not in categories 2 - 9)

    Includes :   disability present but diminishing, and recovery without
                 ultimate restriction in functional performance expected

2   *Improvement potential* (not in categories 3 - 9)

    Includes :   disability present but diminishing, though the individual
                 is likely to be left with residual restriction in functional
                 performance

3   *Assistance potential* (not in categories 4 - 9)

    Includes :   disability in stable or static state, but functional perform-
                 ance could be improved by provision of aids, assistance,
                 or other support

4   *Stable disability* (not in categories 5 - 9)

    Includes :   disability in stable or static state with no outlook for
                 improvement in functional performance

5   *Amelioration potential* (not in categories 6 - 9)

    To ameliorate means to make more bearable

    Includes :   disability increasing, but functional performance could
                 be improved by provision of aids, assistance, or other
                 support

6   *Deteriorating disability* (not in categories 8 or 9)

    Includes :   disability increasing with no outlook for amelioration

8   *Indeterminable outlook*

9   *Outlook unspecified*

Rules for assignment

i   categorize an individual according to the outlook for his activity performance (i.e., disability status), and not for the prognosis of the underlying impairments, other than to the extent that disability may correlate closely with the outlook for the impairments, and taking account of aids and appliances, modification or adaptation of his immediate environment, and assistance received from other persons;

ii   aids or adaptations that it is intended to provide or prescribe should not be taken into account — this would then permit use of the scale as a rough measure of what had been accomplished when such an aid or adaptation was provided;

(Note : the ordination of this scale according to the potential for intervention determines that categories with a potential for assistance or amelioration have lower numbers than the corresponding stable or deteriorating categories — thus provision of assistance or amelioration is likely to lead to reassignment to a category with a higher number, since no further potential for improvement can be assumed)

iii   if doubt is experienced about the category to which a disability should be assigned, rate it to the less favourable category (i.e., that with a higher number)

GUIDANCE ON ASSIGNMENT

To some extent, disabilities can be conceived of in the first instance as threshold phenomena. Thus,to establish the existence and nature of a disability calls only for a judgement about whether a particular accomplishment can be performed or not. In principle, the assignment of failures in accomplishment to the appropriate categories in the code should not prove to be unduly difficult.

The taxonomic structure of the code resembles that of the ICD in that it is hierarchical, with meaning preserved even if the code is used only in abbreviated form. Once again, the level of detail provided is intended to define the content of classes and to allow specificity for users who desire it. However, the scheme is less exhaustive than the I code, and provision has been made for expansion in response to needs uncovered by further experience of applying the code. Thus the level of detail to be recorded is a matter of choice for the user.

Information about major difficulties is generally likely to have been noted in existing records. Coding whatever has been recorded to the appropriate categories of the D code should therefore not present insuperable difficulties. However, two problems should be acknowledged. First, existing records will usually be vulnerable in regard to under-ascertainment — the degree to which significant disabilities may not have been noted. Secondly, some caution is required in connexion with potential variability related to the method of ascertainment. Thus differences are to be expected between assignments based on clinical assessments, functional testing (including the activities of daily living), or questionnaires.

From now on, it is suggested that the major sections of the D code be used as a check-list that is applied to each individual. This would require that the observer ask himself a series of questions ': "Does this person have a behaviour disability, does he have a communication disability, does he have a personal care disability ?" and so on, in sequence. Further information on any question answered affirmatively, along the lines of the greater detail contained in the code, could then be elicited.

Having established the presence of particular disabilities, further questions then arise. This occurs because disability represents a failure in accomplishment, so that a gradation in performance is to be expected. Thus assessment of the severity of individual disabilities is called for. Assessment of outlook is also likely to prove helpful. The basis for such assessments has been indicated on the immediately preceding pages, dealing with supplementary gradings. It is unfortunate that, in attempting retrospective assessment on the basis of existing records, insufficient details of the level of performance may prevent full application of the supplementary gradings.

Two aspects of the D code are likely to command particular attention in the future. First, the proposals in the code contrast fairly markedly with the complexity and exhaustiveness of conventional assessment schedules for the activities of daily living. The difference in approach is based on preliminary reappraisal of goals and methods,[1] and it is hoped that further experience with the code will help resolve the differences in such a way as to promote economy in future assessment effort. Secondly, users have the opportunity to expand the code in order to meet their own needs more satisfactorily. It is hoped that, as requested in the Introduction, such developments will be communicated to the originators of these classifications.

1.   Badley, E.M., Lee, J. & Wood, P.H.N. (1979) *Rheumatology and Rehabilitation*, **18**, 105-109.

SECTION 4

CLASSIFICATION OF HANDICAPS

List of dimensions
1 Orientation handicap
2 Physical independence handicap
3 Mobility handicap
4 Occupation handicap
5 Social integration handicap
6 Economic self-sufficiency handicap
7 Other handicap
Guidance on assessment

HANDICAP

Definition

In the context of health experience, a handicap is a disadvantage for a given individual, resulting from an impairment or a disability, that limits or prevents the fulfilment of a role that is normal (depending on age, sex, and social and cultural factors) for that individual

Characteristics

Handicap is concerned with the value attached to an individual's situation or experience when it departs from the norm. It is characterized by a discordance between the individual's performance or status and the expectations of the individual himself or of the particular group of which he is a member. Handicap thus represents socialization of an impairment or disability, and as such it reflects the consequences for the individual — cultural, social, economic, and environmental — that stem from the presence of impairment and disability

Disadvantage arises from failure or inability to conform to the expectations or norms of the individual's universe. Handicap thus occurs when there is interference with the ability to sustain what might be designated as "survival roles" (see next page)

Classification

It is important to recognize that the handicap classification is neither a taxonomy of disadvantage nor a classification of individuals. Rather is it a classification of circumstances in which disabled people are likely to find themselves, circumstances that place such individuals at a disadvantage relative to their peers when viewed from the norms of society

LIST OF DIMENSIONS OF HANDICAP

SURVIVAL ROLES

1	Orientation handicap
2	Physical independence handicap
3	Mobility handicap
4	Occupation handicap
5	Social integration handicap
6	Economic self-sufficiency handicap

OTHER HANDICAPS

7	Other handicaps

Survival roles The six key dimensions of experience in which competence is expected of the individual have been designated as survival roles. For each of these dimensions the more important array of circumstances that may apply has been scaled. In contrast to the impairment and disability classifications, in which individuals are likely to be identified only in the categories that apply to them, in the handicap classification it is desirable that individuals always be identified on each dimension or survival role. This will provide a profile of their disadvantage status

Other handicaps The six major survival roles by no means exhaust the possibilities of disadvantage, although they do cover the major problems. The varied nature of other handicaps precludes scaling, and so provision has been made just for the identification of these difficulties

1 ORIENTATION HANDICAP

Definition

Orientation is the individual's ability to orient himself in relation to his surroundings

Characteristics

Scale construct : orientation to surroundings, including reciprocation or interaction with surroundings

Includes : reception of signals from surroundings (such as by seeing, listening, smelling, or touching), assimilation of these signals, and expression of response to what is assimilated ; consequences of disabilities of behaviour and communication, and including the planes of seeing, listening, touching, speaking, and assimilation of these functions by the mind

Excludes: response to reception and assimilation of signals from the surroundings manifest as handicaps of personal care (physical independence handicap, 2), evasion of physical hazard (mobility handicap, 3), behaviour in specific situations (occupation handicap, 4), and behaviour towards others (social integration handicap, 5)

Scale categories

0 *Fully oriented* (not in categories 1-9)

1 *Fully compensated impediment to orientation* (not in categories 2-9)

Includes : continuous use of aids for seeing (e.g., spectacles), listening (e.g., amplification), or extension of touching (e.g., a cane), or continuous use of medication to control behaviour or communication disabilities, with resultant restoration of full orientation

Excludes : aids or medication used intermittently (other handicaps, 7)

2 *Intermittent disturbance of orientation* (not in categories 3-9)

Includes : episodic experiences that interfere with full orientation, such as vertigo, those associated with Menieres disease, diplopia (as may be encountered with multiple sclerosis), intermittent interruption of consciousness (e.g., epilepsy), and certain impediments of speech form (e.g., stuttering)

Excludes : fully corrected or controlled disturbances (category 1)

3   *Partially compensated impediment to orientation* (not in categories 4-9)

Includes :   individuals otherwise classifiable to categories 1 or 2 but who experience disadvantage in some aspect of their lives because the impediment to orientation renders them vulnerable in certain circumstances, such as critical dependence on levels of illumination, for some seeing disabilities; critical dependence on levels of background noise and other competing signals, for listening disabilities and some speaking disabilities (e.g., where speech volume is impaired); and disadvantage attributed to the need for aids or medication (e.g., by virtue of resultant ineligibility to take up certain employments or to drive an auto- mobile — code such instances additionally as cur- tailed occupation, category 2, of occupation handi- cap, 4)

4   *Moderate impediment to orientation* (not in categories 5-9)

Includes :   where aids or medication fail to produce satisfactory compensation of the impediment, so that appreciable difficulty in orientation is experienced; or where assistance is required from other people, such as for individuals who are partially sighted, have appreciable hearing loss, have insensitivity to touch, are confused, or have other appreciable impediments

5   *Severe impediments to orientation* (not in categories 6-9)

Includes :   severe behaviour or communication disabilities where substitution is necessary, such as more severe degrees of the states encountered in category 4 (i.e., the indi- vidual cannot perform the activity, even with aid, and so is dependent on substitution by other planes of orientation in order to compensate, such as the reliance of the blind on listening or touching), or moderate disorientation

6   *Orientation deprivation* (not in categories 7-9)

Includes :   where there is moderate or severe impediment in more than one plane of orientation, these planes being seeing, listening, touching, and speaking

Excludes :   disabilities of speech form associated with deafness (assign such individuals solely according to listening status unless speaking disturbance is so severe as to interfere with communication; assign individuals in the latter situation to category 6)

7   *Disorientation* (not in categories 8 or 9)
      Includes : inability of the individual to orient himself to his surroundings to the extent that he requires institutional care

8   *Unconscious*

9   *Unspecified*

Rules for assignment

i   occasional difficulty or dependence on help should not preclude assignment to a less disadvantaged category (i.e., that with a lower number);

ii   aids or adaptations that it is intended to provide or prescribe should not be taken into account — this would then permit use of the classification as a rough measure of what had been accomplished when such an aid or adaptation was provided ;

iii   if doubt is experienced about the category to which an individual should be assigned, rate him to the less favourable category (i.e., that with a higher number);

iv   morale is obviously an important factor, but an individual should be assigned according to his actual degree of dependence, rather than to what the assessor thinks he may be capable of

2   PHYSICAL INDEPENDENCE HANDICAP

Definition

Physical independence is the individual's ability to sustain a customarily effective independent existence

Characteristics

Scale construct :   independence in regard to aids and the assistance of others
Includes :   self-care and other activities of daily living
Excludes :   aids or assistance in orientation (orientation handicap, 1)

Scale categories

0   *Fully independent* (not in categories 1-9)
        Includes :   independence in self-care and without dependence on
                      aids, appliances, environmental modification, or the
                      assistance of other people, or dependent only on minor
                      aids not essential to independence (the latter should
                      be identified as other handicaps, 7)

1   *Aided independence* (not in categories 2-9)
        Assignment to this category depends on the provision and use of
        an aid or appliance. Individuals who have been provided with an
        aid or appliance but do not make use of it, and thus forfeit some
        of their independence, and individuals living in cultures where
        suitable aids and appliances are not available, should be assigned
        to category 3 or 4.
        Includes :   dependence on the use of aids and appliances, such as an
                     artificial or substitute limb, other prostheses, walking
                     aids, or aids to daily living, as well as controlled excretory
                     difficulty
        Excludes :   minor aids and appliances not essential to independence,
                     such as artificial dentures or ring pessaries to control
                     prolapse of the womb, and seeing aids (spectacles) pro-
                     vided that the individual would not otherwise be depen-
                     dent on assistance of the type described in categories 4 -
                     8; individuals whose lives are assisted or improved by
                     minor aids of this type should be assigned to category 0
                     and should also be identified, as appropriate, under
                     orientation (1) or other handicaps (7)

2   *Adapted independence* (not in categories 3-9)
        Assignment to this category presupposes two conditions. First, that
        the immediate environment customary to the way of life of the indi-
        vidual and the group of which he is a member creates physical ob-

stacles to independence, e.g., structural or architectural barriers such as ladders or stairs (for the purpose of this category immediate environment shall be interpreted as the dwelling); and,secondly, that the potential to create or provide an alternative environment is available in that culture. For example, a lake dweller encounters obstacles in climbing a ladder to his dwelling, and yet the means for an alternative environment do not exist in that culture

Includes :   dependence on modification or adaptation of the immediate environment, such as individuals who are dependent on a wheelchair, provided that the individual can get in and out of, operate, and otherwise transfer to and from the chair without assistance from another individual ; individuals who have been re-housed in order to reduce their physical dependence, because of their previous inability to cope with a dwelling of more than one storey ; and individuals who have had structural alterations or special adaptations to their dwellings, such as the provision of a ramp or a lift, or an alteration in the height of working surfaces, etc.

Excludes :   architectural barriers not related to the individual's dwelling (difficulties in this regard should be assigned to category 3 or 4, as appropriate); individuals who decline an offer of a dwelling with amenities that would reduce their physical dependence, who should be assigned to category 3 or 4

3   *Situational dependence* (not in categories 4-9)

Includes :   difficulty in meeting personal needs but without being largely dependent on others, such as may arise because aids and appliances or environmental modifications or adaptations are not feasible or not available within the culture in which the individual lives, or, if available, are declined ; difficulty in mobility outside the home that is overcome only with the assistance of other people ; and moderate impediments to orientation that require assistance from other people

4   *Long-interval dependence* (not in categories 5-9)

Long-interval needs are those that arise once every 24 hours or less frequently

Includes :   dependence on other individuals for meeting long-interval needs such as those identified as subsistence or household disabilities, which relate to the ability to perform tasks necessary for maintenance of acceptable degrees of sustenance, warmth, cleanliness, and security; need for sheltered or supervised accommodation

Excludes : culturally determined dependence, such as the customary dependence of an employed male on his spouse (which in this context shall not be regarded as a disadvantage)

5   *Short-interval dependence* (not in categories 6-9)
Short-interval needs are those that arise every few hours by day

Includes : dependence on other individuals for meeting short-interval needs, such as those identified under personal hygiene, feeding, and other personal care disabilities; mobility within the home; transferring to chair or commode; emptying chamber pot, commode, or bucket; stripping beds and washing linen soiled by urine or faeces; and need for residential care in order to be looked after

6   *Critical-interval dependence* (not in categories 7-9)
Critical-interval needs are those that arise at short and unpredictable intervals by day and which require the continuous availability of help from other persons

Includes : dependence on other individuals for meeting critical-interval needs such as going to the toilet, unfastening and removing clothes, using toilet paper, and cleansing ; individuals who are unable to rise from a bed or chair, walk to the toilet unassisted, use it, and return safely without danger of falling ; and individuals with physical frailty or mental instability giving rise to potential hazard ;
need for institutional care in order to provide supervision, such as for behaviour that is socially unacceptable

7   *Special-care dependence* (not in categories 8 or 9)
Special-care needs are those that arise predominantly throughout the day or throughout the night and that give rise to continuous demands for supervision and help (as opposed to the mere availability of such help, category 6)

Includes : individuals who need someone to supply most of their personal needs and to care for them as far as customary everyday functions are concerned, or are sufficiently senile, or otherwise mentally impaired, to need a similar order of care, and who as a result require the constant attendance of other people thoughout the day; substantial soiling of clothing or bedding by urine or faeces of frequent occurrence other than in response only to physical stress; and individuals who need help with excretory or similar critical functions (such as behaviour) practically every night but who are less dependent by day;
need for institutional care in order to provide restraint of behaviour

8   *Intensive-care dependence*
       Intensive-care needs are those that arise practically every night as
       well as throughout the day and which as a result require the constant
       attendance of other people throughout the 24 hours
       Includes :   individuals who need help with excretory or similar
                    critical functions (such as behaviour) practically every
                    night as well as throughout the day — most individuals
                    in this category need to be fed and dressed, as well as
                    requiring a lot of help during the day with washing and
                    excretory functions, or are incontinent

9   *Unspecified*

Rules for assignment

i   occasional difficulty or dependence on help should not preclude
       assignment to a less disadvantaged category (i.e., that with a lower
       number);

ii   aids or adaptations that it is intended to provide or prescribe should
       not be taken into account — this would then permit use of the classi-
       fication as a rough measure of what had been accomplished when such
       an aid or adaptation was provided ;

iii   if doubt is experienced about the category to which an individual
       should be assigned, rate him to the less favourable category (i.e.,
       that with a higher number);

iv   morale is obviously an important factor, but an individual should be
       assigned according to his actual degree of dependence, rather than to
       what the assessor thinks he may be capable of

3   MOBILITY HANDICAP

Definition

Mobility is the individual's ability to move about effectively in his surroundings

Characteristics

Scale construct : extent of mobility from a reference point, the individual's bed

Includes : the individual's abilities augmented, where appropriate, by prostheses or other physical aids, including a wheelchair (all these should have been identified in categories 1 or 2 of physical independence handicap, 2)

Excludes : mobility attainments with the assistance of other individuals (the latter should be identified as long-interval dependence, category 4 of physical independence handicap, 2)

Scale categories

0   *Fully mobile* (not in categories 1-9)

1   *Variable restriction of mobility* (not in categories 2-9)

Includes : a bronchitic with winter impairment of exercise tolerance, or a severe asthmatic with intermittent impairment of exercise tolerance, and impairments and disabilities following a fluctuating course, such as mild rheumatoid arthritis or (osteo)arthrosis

2   *Impaired mobility* (not in categories 3-9)

Includes : restriction such that the ability to get around is not interfered with but getting around may take longer, e.g., because seeing disability makes the individual uncertain in getting around, or because of other uncertainty, or, in an urbanized society, because the individual has difficulty but nevertheless is able to cope with public transport under all circumstances

3   *Reduced mobility* (not in categories 4-9)

Includes : reduction such that the ability to get around is curtailed, e.g., because seeing disability interferes with the ability to get around; or curtailment because of uncertainty, frailty, or debility; or disability on severe exertion due to cardiac or respiratory impairment; or, in an urbanized society, inability to cope with public transport under all circumstances; or

interference with following occupation by virtue of
difficulty in getting to and from occupation when
this is followed away from the individual's dwelling

4   *Neighbourhood restriction* (not in categories 5-9)
     Includes :   restriction to immediate neighbourhood of dwelling,
              such as by disability on moderate exertion owing to
              cardiac or respiratory impairment

5   *Dwelling restriction* (not in categories 6-9)
     Includes :   confinement to dwelling such as by severe seeing
              disability or disability on mild exertion owing to
              cardiac or respiratory impairment

6   *Room restriction* (not in categories 7-9)
     Includes :   confinement to room, such as by disability at rest
              owing to cardiac or respiratory impairment

7   *Chair restriction* (not in categories 8 or 9)
     Includes :   confinement to chair, such as by disability when
              recumbent owing to cardiac or respiratory
              impairment, or by dependence on hoists or
              similar appliances for getting in and out of bed

8   *Total restriction of mobility*
     Includes :   bedfast or confined to bed

9   *Unspecified*

Rules for assignment

i   categorize an individual according to his independent abilities, taking account of aids and appliances and modification or adaptation of his immediate environment, but disregarding his accomplishments with the aid of other persons (thus uncertainty leading to classification to category 3 or 4 may be reduced in the company of other persons ; this consequential reduction should nevertheless not be taken into account, but the dependence on other persons should be identified under category 3 or 5, as appropriate, of physical independence handicap, 2) ;

ii   occasional reduction or restriction of mobility should not preclude assignment to a less disadvantaged category (i.e., that with a lower number);

iii   aids or adaptations that it is intended to provide or prescribe should not be taken into account ;

iv   if doubt is experienced about the category to which an individual should be assigned, rate him to the less favourable category (i.e., that with a higher number);

v   an individual should be categorized according to his actual degree of mobility, rather than to what the assessor thinks he may be capable of

Notes   a) Problems may be encountered in selecting categories, such as the choice between categories 2 and 3 in areas where a public transport system is not available. In instances like these the individual should be assigned to the less favourable category, in accordance with Rule iv, because it is only by providing a special vehicle that category 2 mobility can be accomplished. This convention should be applied even if the individual's occupation or way of life does not call for overall mobility; it is only the effort that would be deployed in trying to modify his category that would be influenced by these facts

   b) The dependence of disadvantage on cultural norms is well illustrated by a problem in urbanized societies. The behaviour of bus drivers in one area might preclude use of public transport by disabled persons in that area, whereas more sympathetic behaviour by bus drivers in another area might allow someone with the same disability to use public transport. This leads to a conflict between reproducibility (a category meaning the same thing in all places) and the ability of the classification to reflect an individual's needs. The handicap classification is intended predominantly for the latter purpose, and only secondarily for transcultural comparisons

4   OCCUPATION HANDICAP

Definition

Occupation is the individual's ability to occupy his time in the manner customary to his sex, age, and culture

Characteristics

Scale construct : the ability to sustain appropriate occupation of time for
the working day

Includes : play or recreation, employment, and the elderly pursuing
occupations customary to their age group, which in many
cultures includes their assuming a more domestic role and
fulfilling this after the upper age for normal employment

Excludes : restriction or loss of the ability to follow an occupation
that is not due to an individual's impairment, such as
might arise because of changes in employment possibilities

Scale categories

0   *Customarily occupied* (not in categories 1-9)

  Includes : where educational opportunities exist, the ability of a
child to attend a normal school; independent of educational opportunities, the ability of a child to participate in the activities customary for his age group; the
ability to run a household in the accepted manner;
and the ability to discharge the responsibilities customarily expected of a parent bringing up young children

1   *Intermittently unoccupied* (not in categories 2-9)

  Includes : intermittent inability to follow customary occupation
or leisure-time activities, e.g., because of interference
by conditions such as epilepsy, migraine, or allergy,
or because of occasional falls (with or without injury)
in the elderly

2   *Curtailed occupation* (not in categories 3-9)

  Includes : reduced ability to follow customary occupation, such
as in children able to attend normal school but who
suffer from disabilities that restrict participation in
all the activities of the school; individuals who are
unable to participate in all the activities associated
with their customary occupation or recreation (e.g.,
"light work"); and individuals experiencing difficulty in running a household or in discharging the
responsibilities customarily expected of a parent
bringing up young children, although they are able
to manage these activities

3   *Adjusted occupation* (not in categories 4-9)
        Includes :   inability to follow customary occupation,but the
                     individual is able to follow modified or alternative
                     full-time occupation (including modifications to
                     customary occupation because of disability, e.g.,
                     alterations at work place or provision of special
                     assistance or aids); alteration of recreations and
                     other leisure activities (e.g.,hobbies); need for
                     special help at ordinary school (e.g.,because the
                     individual is partially sighted or partially deaf, or
                     because he needs toilet assistance or help with
                     feeding); restriction of career choice because of
                     impairment or disability; necessity to change em-
                     ployment or occupation (including premature re-
                     tirement — after attaining the customary age of
                     retirement the individual should be reassigned to
                     one of the categories 0-2, as appropriate); and
                     having to make special arrangements to allow
                     continued running of household or looking after
                     children (e.g.,by compensatory role adaptation
                     by spouse, by some extra support from social net-
                     work, by special purchase of labour-saving devices,
                     or by employment of some paid assistance with
                     general duties such as cleaning)

4   *Reduced occupation* (not in categories 5-9)
        Includes :   limitations on the amount of time the individual
                     is able to devote to his occupation, such as curtail-
                     ment of recreation and other leisure activities (e.g.,
                     because of conditions such as rheumatic heart disease);
                     able to attend school only part-time, or other re-
                     duction in amount of regular educational instruc-
                     tion; able to sustain only part-time employment or
                     occupation because of impairment or disability;
                     impaired concentration in the elderly (domestic
                     and parental responsibilities can usually be discharged
                     on a more fluid time scale than other occupations,
                     and this may allow compensation for limitations in
                     the time that can be devoted to them — interference
                     with these activities therefore does not feature in
                     this category)

5   *Restricted occupation* (not in categories 6-9)

Includes :   limitations on the type of occupation the individual follows, such as severe restriction of participation in activities customary for the individual's age group; disabilities that preclude a child from attending a normal school (e.g., the need to attend a special establishment for disabled children, where such exists); moderate mental retardation; able to gain employment only under special circumstances (e.g., in a sheltered workshop); has to delegate most of responsibilities for running a household or bringing up children (e.g., by appreciable support from social network or by employment of assistance); and frequent falls in the elderly

6   *Confined occupation* (not in categories 7-9)

Includes :   limitations on both the type of occupation the individual follows and the amount of time he devotes to it, such as inability to participate in activities customary for the individual's age group; disabilities that require a child to be resident in an institution for purposes of education (where such exists), or to be educated at home (where this is not customary); severe mental retardation; able to carry out only very limited domestic activities (e.g.,those connected with running a household or bringing up children); and impairment of concentration leading to difficulty in sustaining an occupation

Excludes :   residence in an institution by virtue of behavioural maladjustment or the need for restraint (categories 5-8 of physical independence handicap, 2)

7   *No occupation* (not in categories 8 or 9)

Includes :   inability to follow occupation because of impairment or disability, such as severe limitation in ability to benefit from educational endeavours (e.g.,profound mental retardation); unable to sustain any form of employment; unable to run a household or bring up children; and severe impairment of concentration leading to inability to sustain an occupation

8   *Unoccupiable*
        Includes :   inability to occupy self in a meaningful manner

9   *Unspecified*

Rules for assignment

i   occasional less favourable experience should not preclude assignment to a less disadvantaged category (i.e., that with a lower number);

ii   if doubt is experienced about the category to which an individual should be assigned, rate him to the less favourable category (i.e., that with a higher number);

iii   an individual should be categorized according to his actual occupation status, rather than to what the assessor thinks he may be capable of

5   SOCIAL INTEGRATION HANDICAP

Definition

Social integration is the individual's ability to participate in and maintain customary social relationships

Characteristics

Scale construct :   individual's level of contact with a widening circle, from the reference point of self

Scale categories

0   *Socially integrated* (not in categories 1-9)
       Includes :   full participation in all customary social relationships

1   *Inhibited participation* (not in categories 2-9)
       Includes :   individuals in whom the presence of an impairment or disability gives rise to nonspecific disadvantage that may inhibit but not prevent participation in the full range of customary social activities (includes embarrassment, shyness, and other defects of self-image due to disfigurement or other impairments and disabilities); and certain mild personality impairments or behaviour disabilities

2   *Restricted participation* (not in categories 3-9)
       Includes :   individuals who do not participate in the full range of customary social activities, such as those with impairments or disabilities that interfere with opportunities for marriage; curtailment of sexual activity because of impairment or disability; and certain personality impairments or behaviour disabilities

       Excludes :   impairments and disabilities that do not interfere with social relationships, such as prolapse of the womb controlled by a ring pessary that does not give rise to appreciable curtailment of sexual activity

3   *Diminished participation* (not in categories 4-9)
       Includes :   individuals who are unable to relate to casual acquaintances, so that social relationships are confined to primary and secondary contacts such as family, friends, neighbours, and colleagues: and individuals who are retarded in physical, psychological, or social development but in whom developmental improvement is continuing

4   *Impoverished relationships* (not in categories 5-9)
        Includes :   individuals who have difficulty in sustaining relations
                     with secondary contacts such as friends, neighbours,
                     and colleagues: and individuals who are retarded in
                     physical, psychological, or social development and
                     in whom there is no evidence that developmental
                     improvement is occurring

5   *Reduced relationships* (not in categories 6-9)
        Includes :   individuals who are able to relate only to significant
                     others, such as parent or spouse; general withdrawal
                     or disengagement by an elderly person; and moder-
                     ately severe behaviour disorders

6   *Disturbed relationships* (not in categories 7-9)
        Includes :   individuals who have difficulty in relating to signifi-
                     cant others; and severe behaviour disorders

7   *Alienated* (not in categories 8 or 9)
        Includes :   individuals who are unable to relate to other people;
                     impairment or disability preventing the development
                     of normal social relationships; and individuals in whom
                     behavioural maladjustment prevents coexistence and
                     integration in the customary home and family; and
                     elderly persons following the loss of family and
                     friends and with reduced capacity to enter into new
                     relationships

8   *Socially isolated*
        Includes :   individuals whose capacity for social relationships is
                     indeterminable because of their isolated situation,
                     such as those admitted to institutional care because
                     of lack of social support in the home or community
                     (e.g., children in an orphanage or otherwise aban-
                     doned, and residents in an old people's home)

9   *Unspecified*

Rules for assignment

i   occasional reduction in social integration should not preclude
        assignment to a less disadvantaged category (i.e., that with a
        lower number);

ii   if doubt is experienced about the category to which the indi-
        vidual should be assigned, rate him to the less favourable cat-
        egory (i.e., a higher number);

iii   an individual should be categorized according to his actual degree of social integration, rather than to what the assessor thinks he may be capable of

6 ECONOMIC SELF-SUFFICIENCY HANDICAP

Definition

Economic self-sufficiency is the individual's ability to sustain customary socioeconomic activity and independence

Characteristics

Scale construct : fundamentally related to economic self-sufficiency, from the reference point of zero economic resources, but, unlike with the other handicap scales, the construct has been extended so as to include possession or command of an unusual abundance of resources; the justification for this extension is the potential that abundant resources provide for relieving or ameliorating disadvantage in other dimensions

Includes : the individual's self-sufficiency in regard to obligations to sustain others, such as members of the family; economic self-sufficiency sustained by virtue of any compensation or standard disability, invalidity, or retirement pension that the individual receives or to which he may be entitled, but excluding any supplementary allowances or benefits to which the individual's poverty may entitle him; economic self-sufficiency by virtue of income (earned or otherwise) or material possessions such as natural resources, livestock, or crops; and poverty resulting from or exacerbated by impairment or disability

Excludes : economic deprivation due to factors other than impairment or disability

Scale categories

0 *Wealthy* (not in categories 1-9)
Includes : individuals in possession of resources considerably in excess of those available to the majority of the population of which the individual forms a part

1 *Comfortably off* (not in categories 2-9)
Includes : individuals in possession of resources sufficiently in excess of their requirements for sustaining their accustomed style of living that the additional resource expenditure incurred in attempts to ameliorate handicap and disability can be accommodated without appreciable sacrifice

2 *Fully self-sufficient* (not in categories 3-9)
   Includes : economic self-sufficiency without support from or
   dependence on financial or material aid from other
   individuals or the community (including the state,
   but compensation or standard disability, invalidity,
   or retirement pensions shall be regarded as income
   entitlement rather than aid in this context) and such
   that the burden of attempts to ameliorate handicap
   and disability can be accommodated without appreciable deprivation

3 *Adjusted self-sufficiency* (not in categories 4-9)
   Includes : individuals who, although economically self-sufficient, have suffered a reduction in economic well-.
   being when compared with status before impairment
   or disability developed or that expected if the individual were not impaired or disabled, such as those
   who have experienced lower economic reward as a
   consequence of having had to change their occupation, or those who have incurred extra expenses because of their disability and to such a degree as to
   lead to appreciable deprivation

4 *Precariously self-sufficient* (not in categories (5-9)
   Includes : individuals who, following a reduction in economic
   well-being, remain self-sufficient only by virtue of
   appreciable support from or dependence on financial or material aid from other individuals or the
   community (including the state, such as an allow-
   ance or benefit supplementary to the customary
   provisions for disability or retirement pensions to
   which they are entitled), and who in the process
   may jeopardize their family's self-sufficiency or
   cause other family members to be deprived

5 *Economically deprived* (not in categories 6-9)
   Includes : individuals who economically are only partially
   self-sufficient because their income or possessions
   or financial or material aid from other individuals
   or the community meets only part of their needs,
   and who in the process may reduce their family
   to a subsistence level of existence

6   *Impoverished* (not in categories 7-9)

        Includes :   Individuals who economically are not self-sufficient by virtue of being totally dependent for financial or material aid on the goodwill of other individuals or the community, because of ineligibility for or non-availability of disablement or retirement pensions or supplementary benefits, and who in the process may reduce their family to existence below subsistence level; or individuals residing in institutions for the indigent

7   *Destitute* (not in categories 8 or 9)

        Includes :   individuals who economically are not self-sufficient and to whom support from others is not available, so that their disability status is further aggravated

8   *Economically inactive*

        Includes :   individuals without family support who are unable to undertake economic activity by virtue of limited competence (such as that resulting from mental retardation) or.tender years (such as a child that has not passed the customary age at which he normally becomes independent of the family for complete economic or material support)

        Excludes :   those with family support and those often regarded as being economically inactive by virtue of their "dependent" status, such as a spouse or other cohabitant (assign to one of the categories 0-7, as appropriate, according to economic self-sufficiency of family or head of family)

9   *Unspecified*

Rules for assignment

i   categorize an individual according to the economic self-sufficiency of his family, so that dependent status is not taken into account;

ii   occasional reduction in economic self-sufficiency should not preclude assignment to a less disadvantaged category (i.e., that with a lower number);

iii   pensions or supplementary benefits that it is intended to provide or prescribe should not be taken into account;

iv   if doubt is experienced about the category to which an individual should be assigned, rate him to the less favourable category (i.e., that with a higher number)

7   OTHER HANDICAPS

Definition

Other circumstances that may give rise to disadvantage

Characteristics

Excludes :   disadvantages identified elsewhere in the handicap
              classification

Categories

0   *Not subject to disadvantage*
        Includes :   impairments or disabilities not giving rise to appreci-
                     able disadvantage, such as some chronic diseases that
                     do not appreciably interfere with everyday life

1   *Minor disadvantage*
        Includes :   the need to use minor aids that do not appreciably
                     interfere with everyday life, such as dentures, reading
                     glasses, or a ring pessary to control uterine prolapse;
                     intermittent use of aids or medication to control
                     disability

2   *Nonspecific disadvantage*
        Includes :   impairments or disabilities that give rise to general or
                     nonspecific disadvantage, such as coeliac disease or the
                     state of being delicate

3   *Specific disadvantage*
        Includes :   reduction of the quality of life as a result of specific
                     disadvantage not elsewhere identified in the handicap
                     classification

9   *Unspecified disadvantage*

GUIDANCE ON ASSESSMENT

The structure of the H code is radically different from that of all other ICD-related classifications. Thus the codes are not hierarchical in the customarily accepted sense, and abbreviation is not really acceptable. What is called for is that every individual should be categorized according to each dimension of the H code, the latter relating to various circumstances in which disabled people are likely to find themselves. As a result of these considerations, the difficulties in applying the H code relate not to assignment, but to assessment of the individual's status in regard to each dimension of handicap. However, the basis for such assessments has been indicated under each of the dimensions.

For retrospective application to existing records, the major difficulty is likely to be incomplete information. Nevertheless, as noted in the Introduction, the orientation of whatever information may be available to the dimensions of the H code can still be very instructive.

From now on, it is hoped that information will be gathered so as to permit assessment in each dimension of the code. The main aspect likely to command attention in the future relates to the development of assessment schedules. These are likely to be based on a questionnaire approach, so that problems with language will loom large, and so it will not be easy to develop instruments capable of transcultural application.